Lancashire
County Council

England's Cathedrals by Train

IN MEMORY OF

WILLIAM PICKERING,
who died Dec.ᴿ 24. 1845
AGED 30 YEARS

ALSO RICHARD EDGER
who died Dec.ᴿ 24. 1845.
AGED 24 YEARS.

THE SPIRITUAL RAILWAY

The Line to heaven by Christ was made
With heavenly truth the Rails are laid.
From Earth to Heaven the Line extends.
To Life Eternal where it ends
Repentance is the Station then
Where Passengers are taken in
No Fee for them is there to pay
For Jesus is himself the way
God's Word is the first Engineer
It points the way to Heaven so dear.
Through tunnels dark and dreary here
It does the way to Glory steer.
God's Love the Fire, his Truth the Steam,
Which drives the Engine and the Train,
All you who would to Glory ride,
Must come to Christ, in him abide
In First and Second, and Third Class,
Repentance, Faith and Holiness.
You must the way to Glory gain
Or you with Christ will not remain
Come then poor Sinners, now's the time
At any Station on the Line.
If you'll repent and turn from sin
The Train will stop and take you in.

Ely Cathedral,
Tombstone in South Porch

Tombstone in Ely Cathedral.

England's Cathedrals
by Train

Discover how the Normans and the
Victorians helped to shape our lives

Murray Naylor

First published in Great Britain in 2013 by
Remember When
an imprint of
Pen & Sword Books Ltd
47 Church Street
Barnsley
South Yorkshire
S70 2AS

ISBN 978 1 78303 028 6

A CIP catalogue record for this book is available from the British Library

Typeset in Ehrhardt by
Mac Style, Bridlington, East Yorkshire
Printed and bound in India by Replika Press Pvt. Ltd.

Pen & Sword Books Ltd incorporates the imprints of Pen & Sword Archaeology,
Atlas, Aviation, Battleground, Discovery, Family History, History, Maritime,
Military, Naval, Politics, Railways, Select, Social History, Transport, True Crime, and
Claymore Press, Frontline Books, Leo Cooper, Praetorian Press, Remember When,
Seaforth Publishing and Wharncliffe.

For a complete list of Pen & Sword titles please contact
PEN & SWORD BOOKS LIMITED
47 Church Street, Barnsley, South Yorkshire, S70 2AS, England
E-mail: enquiries@pen-and-sword.co.uk
Website: www.pen-and-sword.co.uk

Contents

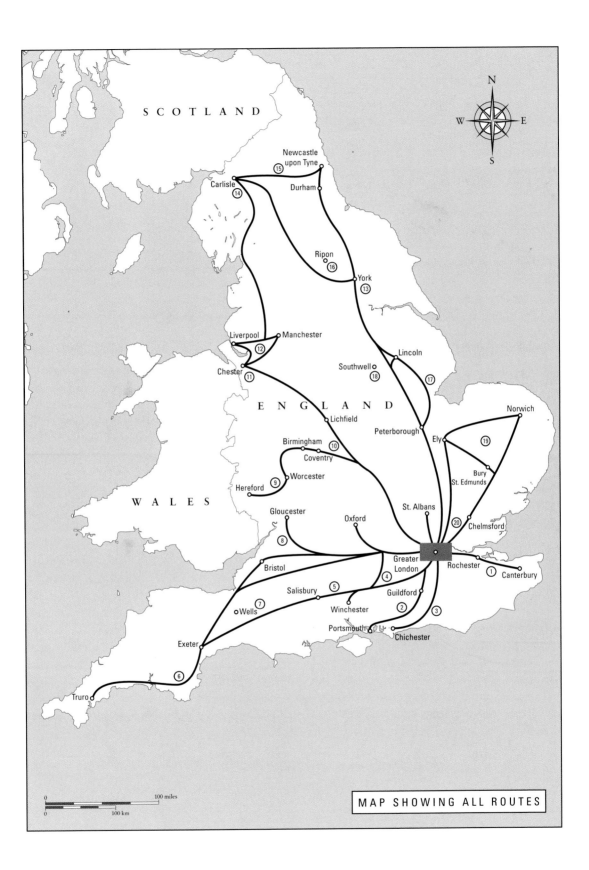

MAP SHOWING ALL ROUTES

Foreword

by the Rt Revd and Rt Hon The Lord Hope of Thornes KCVO

It was in the course of my sermon during my enthronement as Archbishop of York in 1995 that I remarked that in my younger days I would no doubt have been more interested in *Mallard* in the Railway Museum than Walter de Grey in the minster. No such dilemma for Murray Naylor, who in this remarkable book manages to weave together both railways and cathedrals in a fascinating and captivating way.

Reading through the book brought back some happy memories of trainspotting on Doncaster Station in my younger days with those Ian Allan books and photographs by the 'railway bishop', Eric Treacy, one of my predecessors in the See of Wakefield – a diocese itself established mainly because it was on the main line to London. It was perhaps ironic that Treacy should have collapsed and died on Appleby Station on the approach of a steam train on the Settle-Carlisle line, with now a plaque to mark the spot. And now, myself retired and living almost alongside the Settle-Carlisle Railway, it's an enormous thrill still to see the steam-hauled excursion trains as they pass by within a few yards of my home.

The journeys Murray Naylor describes take the reader the length and breadth of the country with descriptions of the respective cathedrals as erudite as they are accessible, though it has to be said the week-long journey outlined in order to make visits to all the cathedrals mentioned left me feeling somewhat breathless.

In addition to the wise guidance for the visitor to the cathedrals, highlighting as the author does the main features of the building, he also includes some of the people and stories associated with them and not least the visionary impetus of some of the bishops.

Yet here is no 'museum-type' guide. For certainly the historic and architectural features are full of fascination and interest, and generally Naylor gives the reader as much as is necessary. He also recognizes that they are places of life and vigour still (cathedrals are as well maintained as they ever have been, and at considerable cost to the church in spite of substantial grant aid; they are also enjoying something of a renaissance given the rising number of worshippers attending), as day by day and week by week they have kept alive the very reason for which they were built in the first place – the worship of God, reflecting as they do the grandeur and splendour of the kingdom of heaven. The words of the Puritan poet John Milton spring to mind:

> *But let my due feet never fail*
> *To walk the studious cloister's pale,*
> *And love the high embowered roof,*
> *With antique pillars massy proof,*
> *And storied windows richly dight,*

Casting a dim religious light.
There let the pealing organ blow,
To the full voiced choir below …
As may with sweetness through mine ear,
Dissolve me into ecstasies,
And bring all heaven before mine eyes.

Extract from *Il Penseroso*, 1631

The 'railway notes' too are equally instructive and full of interest, telling as they do the sometimes extraordinary lengths to which the Victorians went to build up so comprehensive a network of lines, many of them coming at considerable cost to the workforce – again one of the most notorious of the projects being the construction of the Settle-Carlisle line over Blea Moor, still as bleak and unyielding on a stormy day today as it was then. It is clear that Naylor's enthusiasm for the cathedrals is well matched by his enthusiasm for the railways and his detailed knowledge too of some of the more technical aspects of rail engineering and operating add greatly to the reader's interest, as does the commentary on the development and demise of particular lines and routes.

In all, here is a book that is as instructive as it is accessible, containing as it does both learning and personal story, which combine to celebrate two of the greatest achievements of these islands – cathedrals and railways – all of which makes for a compelling read. Journeys are at the heart of both the railways and the Christian faith and life, as is well exemplified by *The Spiritual Railway*, which forms the frontispiece of this book. Hopefully the reader will discover the pleasure and the reward of the journey that this book so readily offers.

David, Lord Hope of Thornes KCVO

List of Illustrations

The Author has taken all possible steps to check the architectural and chronological details given in the book. He accepts responsibility for any inaccuracies that remain.

Unless otherwise stated, all illustrations have been provided by the author.

Author's Note

In seeking to combine under a single title a study of cathedrals and how to reach them using Britain's railway system, I should perhaps explain why I have not included descriptions of all forty-three Anglican cathedrals. Some cathedrals were built to be cathedrals from the beginning, examples of these being the magnificent medieval buildings at York, Salisbury and Lincoln. Others started life as medieval churches or monastic settlements, which later became cathedrals as populations grew and more dioceses were required to minister to the needs of parishes and their congregations. Examples include the present-day cathedrals at Newcastle and Chelmsford. In recording my observations of the cathedrals selected, I have confined my descriptions to aspects of a building that attracted my attention and that I believe will interest a visitor who may have limited time at his or her disposal. If as a result I have omitted details others might feel to be important, then I can but apologize.

No discourtesy is intended to cathedrals not selected. In particular, I have not included the cathedrals in London. As explained in 'The Journey' introduction, the magnificence and importance of Westminster Abbey and St Paul's Cathedral alone merit their being visited outside the confines of this book. However, every rule has its exceptions and I have included four cathedrals completed in more modern times: Truro, built in the late nineteenth century; Liverpool and Guildford, both finished in the latter half of the twentieth century; and Coventry, reconstructed following the total devastation of the previous cathedral in the Second World War. In my opinion all deserve inclusion either for the achievements of their builders or their contribution to Christian culture.

I have applied similar criteria when describing operational railway issues or aspects of railway routes linking selected cathedrals. Some of the information provided is common to a number of routes and topics and it would be monotonous to repeat it in every instance where the same rail journey may be followed, albeit to a different destination. Equally, some descriptions apply only to one route, such as the narrative in Chapter 6 describing the role played by the renowned Victorian railway engineer Isambard Kingdom Brunel in developing Cornwall's railways. It is clearly impossible to record all aspects of railway operations in a book of this size and I trust the reader will enjoy my chosen observations and be informed by them. Cross-referencing is included where appropriate to link a person or an event appearing in two or more places.

All journeys start from London. They radiate clockwise around the country beginning in the south-east with a journey to Canterbury and culminating in visits to St Albans and Chelmsford, having gone west as far as Truro, north to Carlisle and east to Norwich.

Murray Naylor
Malton, North Yorkshire, 2013

Preface

Stone and Steam

The Normans built great castles and fine churches after William the Conqueror's invasion of 1066. Their purpose was to consolidate William's rule and leave the population in no doubt that the Normans were here to stay. This they did very successfully. Over the intervening 950 years their medieval cathedrals have been enhanced and, in some places, replaced by new versions in similar or different styles. Since the Reformation cathedrals have reflected the spiritual leadership of the Anglican Church and are today probably better respected and more frequently visited by greater numbers of people than ever before. They stand, centuries after construction, as places of worship, pilgrimage and wonder in a world where the importance of history is all too often forgotten or overlooked.

Eight hundred years after William landed in Britain the Victorians set about finding ways to make travel more efficient and less hazardous. Men like James Watt, the Stephensons, Isambard Kingdom Brunel and others created a railway system that gave Britain and, later, the world, a means of transport unrivalled until the invention of the automobile and the aeroplane. Locomotives, iron rails and civil engineering structures have all been developed since the mid-nineteenth century to provide a system that still endures in much the same basic form as when first created. Railways permit people to travel quickly and in relative comfort and there is no indication that this will change, in the immediate future, anyway. Ever more crowded commuter trains, an apparently unquenchable desire for long-distance surface travel increasingly by rail rather than by road and a growing realization of the damage that fossil fuels can cause to the environment combine to assure rail travel an expanding future.

The idea of linking cathedrals and railways in one book is based upon a wish to draw attention to what these two great human achievements have in common. While there may be no immediately discernible symmetry between the two they both reflect the ingenuity of mankind. They clearly complement one another in that the one can be used to reach the other. Cathedrals could be said to be historically immoveable objects in the world of the civil engineer while railways have, quite literally, always been an irresistible force.

I have lived with and travelled on railways all my life and am an advocate of their greater use, while visiting England's magnificent cathedrals never fails to revitalize my inner spirit. A personal belief tells me that the older we become the greater the need to return to our roots. Linking these two subjects in one book has allowed me to extol the contribution made by England's cathedrals and her railways to our national heritage and, in doing so, encourage readers to undertake journeys similar to those I have made myself.

Scarborough Spa Express. Locomotive *Scots Guardsman*.

The Journey

Y ou can begin the journey anywhere, stop it anywhere and finish it anywhere. You can undertake it in one sweep or in a number of separate excursions, either in a single day or over a number of days. You can do it as fast or as slowly as you wish. It matters not.

If you have a choice, start in London in Parliament Square. By all means look at the sights around you – Big Ben, the Houses of Parliament, the Cenotaph, and the more distant prospect of Nelson's Column towering over Trafalgar Square – but above all rest your gaze upon Westminster Abbey, one of the oldest of our great churches, built by King Edward the Confessor and consecrated eight days before his death in 1065. Here is a church that embodies the Christian spirit of Britain. Beneath its ancient stones are buried monarchs, statesmen, explorers, soldiers and poets while its precincts have witnessed coronations, national celebrations of thanksgiving, weddings and funerals. If any church can be said to represent the religious heart of Britain it is Westminster Abbey. It reflects the history of our islands in a way no other building can equal.

The abbey is not included in this book since its history and splendour are so well recorded elsewhere, as indeed are those of London's other great church, St Paul's Cathedral, a few miles to the east of Westminster. This book is instead about England's cathedrals in the provinces outside London, many of which can rival Westminster Abbey and St Paul's Cathedral in their beauty, history and traditions.

Having savoured the glories of the abbey, go to the London terminus appropriate to your first journey and begin your travels. Paddington, St Pancras, King's Cross and Waterloo stations, to name but four, built by the Victorians, with their wide concourses and wonderfully engineered and lofty, curved roofs, cathedral-like in their architecture, symbolize the transience of the journey, while the silence and stillness of our cathedrals exemplify the permanence and peace of arrival. This book invites you to travel through these stations to discover how cathedrals built by our Norman ancestors and by others since have sustained the Christian faith over the ages.

South East

Canterbury Cathedral.

The nave, Canterbury Cathedral.

Chapter 1

Canterbury and Rochester

■ Commuting by rail ■ the High Speed One Route ■ the Channel Tunnel
■ **Canterbury Cathedral** ■ St Augustine ■ **Rochester Cathedral**
■ the Romney, Hythe & Dymchurch Railway ■

Getting There

You have a choice of two modes of travel. The first is to go to St Pancras International Station and take the high-speed Javelin service to Canterbury West, a journey of one hour. This route, which is more expensive than the alternatives, follows the High Speed One (HS1) line (explained below) to the Channel Tunnel as far as Ashford, where it diverges onto the classic third rail line to Canterbury.

After visiting Canterbury Cathedral you can take a second classic service of no more than thirty minutes duration from Canterbury East to Rochester. Following a visit to the cathedral there, you should then join a Southeastern Javelin service to return to St Pancras, a journey of little more than thirty minutes.

The alternative would be not to use an HS1 service but to travel throughout on a classic service from Victoria, Charing Cross, Waterloo East or London Bridge stations. Services from all these stations are frequent but take considerably longer than those provided by high-speed Javelin trains.

Railway Notes

People living in Kent have long wished for more efficient rail communications to London. Although in recent years efforts have been made to speed up services, trains from Ramsgate, Dover and the Medway towns can take as long to reach the capital as those from towns to the north and west of London that cover twice the distance. For many commuters who work in the capital this disparity in journey times can be frustrating, especially if trains are delayed. Services along the North Kent coast and from other parts of the county and neighbouring Sussex tend to serve many communities and stops are frequent, while the infrastructure is so intensively used that there always exists the possibility of disruption. Critics of railway services provided in the Home Counties have existed ever since their inception, one of the earliest lines to reach Kent – the London, Chatham and Dover Railway – being nicknamed 'The London, Smash 'em and Turnover' on account of its poor safety record.

However, railway developments at an international level are now bringing relief for the Kent commuter. The building of a rail tunnel under the sea between Britain and France, completed in 1994, and the subsequent creation of a high-speed line to London have not only connected Britain into the European rail network but have resulted in the development of faster domestic services. Opened in November 2007, the high-speed line through Kent connects St Pancras to the Channel Tunnel, a distance of 68 miles. To date, this route – designated High Speed One

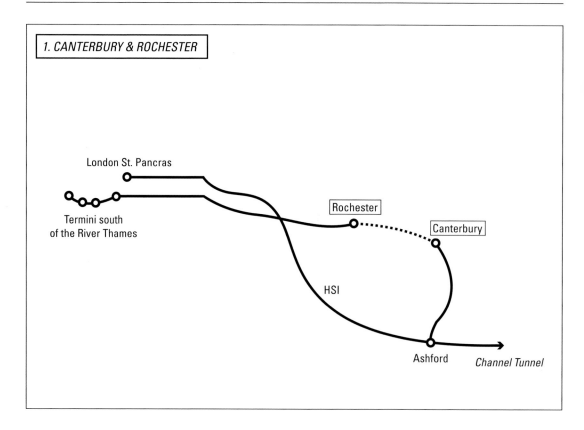

1. CANTERBURY & ROCHESTER

London St. Pancras

Termini south
of the River Thames

Rochester

Canterbury

HS1

Ashford   Channel Tunnel

(HS1) to differentiate it from any similar lines that may be built in the future – is only traversed by Eurostar international passenger services to France and Belgium and some freight traffic, but it may not be long before Continental train operators will be permitted to access London using the link.

Meanwhile, since 2009 some domestic services have been permitted to run on HS1. As a result Javelin trains can travel at speeds of up to 140mph between St Pancras and Ashford or Ebbsfleet, where they diverge from HS1 onto classic third rail lines to reach destinations such as Dover, Ramsgate and Canterbury. In time these hybrid 'fast' services may be extended to serve other destinations, further improving the life of travellers from Kent.

While none of the journeys in this book involve a passage through the Channel Tunnel you may be interested in a brief history of this project. For more than two centuries the practicality of building a fixed link between Britain and France has been debated but it was not until 1988 that, following political accord between the two countries, work finally began to engineer a tunnel linking Folkestone and Calais. Completed in six years and at a length of 31 miles, the tunnel is the second-longest in the world and runs under the sea for a greater distance than any equivalent construction. It is managed by Eurotunnel, a multinational commercial company, and carries not only international passenger and freight traffic but also a shuttle service conveying road vehicles the short transit between the two countries.

Despite problems of financing during the construction period, perceived high transit charges and, more recently, damage caused by fire and disruption by refugees attempting to enter Britain

Eurostar train at St Pancras International Station. (NRM)

Javelin train at Chatham.

illegally, the tunnel is seen as a growing asset. The future offers the prospect of increased traffic as services from Britain connect to further destinations on the Continent, something that in 2006 the European Railway Agency was established to encourage. Meanwhile, in 1996 the American Society of Civil Engineers voted the Channel Tunnel 'one of the seven wonders of the modern world'.

Prior to the completion of the fixed link, rail traffic entering Europe from Britain had to use train ferries to cross the Channel. These vessels provided a useful if restricted means of sea transit but they eventually fell victim to competition from airlines and car ferries as greater numbers of people opted for holidays on the Continent.

My first experience of travelling on a Javelin train occurred when I visited Canterbury and Rochester for this book. The trains are impressive; they ride well and are quiet. The changeover from collecting electric current from overhead transmission wires to drawing it from the third rail system goes unnoticed. The differences between these two systems of current collection are briefly discussed in Chapter 2.

Canterbury Cathedral

The Mother Church of English Christianity.

Look for the place of martyrdom of Thomas Becket, the Black Prince's tomb and St Augustine's Chair.

Canterbury Cathedral tells the story of Christianity in England from the time of St Augustine's arrival in Kent in the late sixth century. It is therefore only appropriate that my first visit to an Anglican cathedral should be to Canterbury.

It was in 597 that King Ethelbert of Kent, the first of the kings of Anglo-Saxon Britain to embrace the Christian faith, was baptized by St Augustine. Earlier, Augustine had been dispatched from Rome by Pope Gregory the Great with the mission of bringing Christianity to England, at that time a predominantly pagan country. Doubtful of their reception, Augustine and his accompanying monks were at first reluctant to cross the Channel from France but their reception in Canterbury, a city originally built as a Roman trading settlement, reinforced their confidence and led to the eventual spreading of the Christian faith throughout the British Isles. Christian worship has taken place at Canterbury ever since.

While Pope Gregory originally envisaged two archbishoprics in England – at London and York – it was later decided that Canterbury should be substituted for London. The cathedral is the seat of the Archbishop of Canterbury, today the head of the Church of England as the Primate of all England and the leader of the worldwide Anglican Communion. However, the archbishop's position as the undisputed leader of the Church has not always been acknowledged and up until the fourteenth century there was bitter rivalry between the two archbishops. How this matter was resolved is related in Chapter 13.

Entering the cathedral by the south-west door the visitor immediately finds himself in the nave. Begun in 1377, the nave literally reaches to the sky and is remarkable for its tall columns, 80 feet in height, which culminate in roof vaulting crowned with a series of bosses. The nave took twenty-eight years to build and is divided from the quire by a screen, or *pulpitum*. Carved on this screen are effigies of six English kings, not unlike those of the fifteen monarchs to be found on the screen in York Minster. Other figures of Christ and his apostles were destroyed in 1643 at the time of the Civil War. Henry Yevele designed the nave, having previously undertaken similar work at Westminster Abbey. The nave windows contain only clear glass, the original stained glass having been destroyed during either the Reformation or the Civil War. Fires following the completion of the work also caused several changes but Yevele's original design remains.

The fabric of many of England's medieval cathedrals sustained calamitous damage when parts of their structures collapsed, either because too much weight was loaded onto unstable foundations or when a natural disaster occurred. Towers were particularly prone to collapse and the Perpendicular-period Bell Harry Tower at Canterbury, completed in 1498 to replace the original Romanesque tower, is strengthened by relieving arches in the nave that help to brace the structure. The tower houses a single bell, installed by Prior Harry Eastry to summon the monastic community to prayer, while the main bells are located in the cathedral's two western towers.

The west end and Bell Harry Tower, Canterbury Cathedral.

Looking east towards St Augustine's Chair, Canterbury Cathedral.

On the north side of the nave in the side aisle is the highly decorated baptismal font given by Charles I and subsequently hidden from the Puritans during the Civil War; it was restored to its original position in 1663.

It is the murder of Thomas Becket in 1170 with which most people will associate Canterbury. Thomas, a close adviser to Henry II and his archbishop, fell out with the king over the issue of the Church's independence from control by the state. Becket's stance so infuriated Henry that the latter publicly called for the primate's removal, following which four knights are said to have accepted the king's challenge, ridden to Canterbury, sought out Thomas and then violently murdered him in the cathedral. The place of the murder is marked with a modern memorial (two ragged steel swords and a broken sword point) called The Martyrdom at the north-east end of the nave and close to one of the entrances to the crypt. Thomas's burial place is unknown and his shrine in the Trinity Chapel was demolished on the orders of Henry VIII in 1538. Thomas's murder and his martyrdom have since the twelfth century been the focus for countless pilgrimages to Canterbury and millions of people must have visited the cathedral in the intervening time. Geoffrey Chaucer's work *Canterbury Tales*, written in the fourteenth century, records the journey of a particular group of pilgrims travelling on foot from London to visit Thomas's shrine.

Following a fire the interior of the Early Gothic quire was rebuilt beginning in 1174 by William of Sens, a French architect who died during its construction when he fell from scaffolding. His work was then taken forward by William the Englishman, who completed the eastern end of the cathedral and built the Trinity Chapel as the shrine to St Thomas Becket. Beyond the high altar between the presbytery and the corona stands St Augustine's Chair, assembled in the thirteenth century and used ever since during the ceremony to enthrone a new archbishop.

There are a large number of tombs in the cathedral, including those of more than fifty archbishops, while Henry IV and his wife are also buried there. Of particular historical interest is the tomb of Edward the Black Prince, Edward III's eldest son, situated on the south side of the Trinity Chapel. He lived during the fourteenth century and spent much of his life fighting the French during the Hundred Years War, dying at the early age of forty-six. He was nicknamed the 'Black Prince' not because of the colour of his armour or equipment but more possibly for the ferocious attitude he adopted in battle, one that is said to have struck fear into the hearts of his opponents.

The early building of the cathedral was undertaken by Archbishop Lanfranc in 1070; all that remains of his original church is part of the crypt, the largest cathedral crypt in the world, as well as some of the cloister walls. Canterbury is also renowned for its medieval glass, much of it dating from the twelfth century. Various windows tell the story of Christianity, the Great West Window depicting Adam tilling the land after being ejected from the Garden of Eden while the principal window in the south-west transept shows some of Christ's ancestors. These include Methuselah, recorded in the Hebrew bible as the oldest man ever and said to have lived for 969 years. St Anselm's Chapel off the south quire aisle contains an altar created by Stephen Cox built in 1959

Tomb of the Black Prince, Canterbury Cathedral.

11

using French Aosta marble. A striking modern window depicts Anselm, who succeeded Lanfranc as archbishop and was responsible for the original quire. He died in 1109.

A visit to Canterbury in the early summer when the narrow streets and the cathedral precincts are thronged with visitors, many of them schoolchildren learning about Christianity and how it took root in England 2,000 years ago, reminded me that the city and its cathedral have long been a destination for pilgrims from all over the world. The Bell Harry Tower and the fine lines of the cathedral provide a stunning spectacle as you approach or leave by train across the North Downs.

Rochester Cathedral

A city associated with more than 1,400 years of Christian worship and with close links to Charles Dickens.

Look for Bishop Gundulf's statue at the west front and the thirteenth-century Wheel of Fortune wall painting in the quire.

Half-an-hour west of Canterbury lie the four towns clustered around the mouth of the river Medway. Of the four, the oldest is Rochester, where there has been a settlement since before Roman times. Its strategic importance as a crossing point over the river on the route from London to Dover was not lost on the early Roman settlers who built a walled city there, followed many years later by an imposing castle constructed by the Normans.

The name of Charles Dickens is associated with Rochester and the town is mentioned in his novels more often than any place except London. Both *The Pickwick Papers* and *Great Expectations* are thought to contain references to Rochester buildings, while each year the town stages an annual Dickens Festival to remember the famous author.

Rochester Cathedral was begun in 604 on the instructions of St Augustine, only a few years after he and his followers had landed in Kent and settled at Canterbury. Rochester was the second bishopric to be established in England, with Justus, the first bishop, being consecrated by Augustine about the same time as the building of the cathedral began. That church was later severely damaged by the Vikings, the next wave of invaders to come to Britain, and it was not until the Normans arrived from France in the eleventh century that the present building was begun.

It was in the early seventh century that Christianity began to percolate across the northern parts of Britain, spearheaded by missionaries like Paulinus, archbishop of the northern province based upon York. However, his strenuous efforts to convert people to Christianity suffered a severe setback in 633 when pagan forces once again overran large tracts of northern Britain, forcing him and his followers to flee south. Later, Paulinus was appointed bishop at Rochester, where his *palium*, or archiepiscopal vestment, was later laid up as a holy relic. Paulinus's importance as an early missionary is recorded in many of our cathedrals.

Bishop Gundulf was appointed by the Normans in 1077 to take the work of building a cathedral forward and, using his not inconsiderable skills as an architect, he played a key role in designing and overseeing construction of the nave and west front, both of which were completed before his death. During this time a community of Benedictine monks was established at Rochester. The Norman cathedral was consecrated in 1130 with Henry I present.

Rochester Cathedral.

During the twelfth century two major fires ravaged the cathedral and the nave and west front were both rebuilt in the Romanesque style. Looting took place in 1215 when King John's forces were billeted in the nave while besieging rebel barons in the castle, and again in 1264 when Simon de Montfort led a national uprising against Henry III, on that occasion the troops defending the castle being loyal to the Crown.

After the traumatic events of the twelfth century the cathedral was gradually developed, with a tower being built in the 1340s and clerestory windows being added in the middle of the fifteenth century to allow more light to enter the building. In the same century, the Lady chapel was added. However, the sixteenth and seventeenth centuries saw fresh upheavals when changes caused by the Reformation and, a hundred years later, during Cromwell's brief period of republican rule, led to the destruction or damaging of priceless artefacts in many church buildings. In 1535, Bishop Fisher, previously Bishop of Rochester, was executed by Henry VIII for failing to support his claim to be the rightful head of the English Church. Twenty years later, Henry's daughter, Queen Mary, ordered that Nicholas Ridley, another former bishop of the diocese, should be burned at the stake for his refusal to accept her plan to return England to Catholic rule. Such were the hazards of autocratic rule by the monarchy in Tudor times.

The quire contains some of the original stalls while a medieval wall painting depicting the Wheel of Fortune, symbolizing man's ambitious quest for money, power and status, has survived although partially obliterated in the 1640s. The walls of the quire are decorated with the royal

The nave, Rochester Cathedral.

leopard of England and the fleur-de-lys of France, intended to make the point that England and France should be ruled by one king, the King of England. At the time, the Hundred Years War was raging.

Rochester Cathedral is one of the oldest in England and has experienced greater turmoil and change than most other cathedrals. Situated close to the ruins of the Norman castle with which it has shared so many historical events, it sits in a tranquil corner of a city that has few other architectural features of which to boast. First impressions are that Rochester Cathedral is a rather sombre place but history soon begins to have its effect as you learn about the cathedral's role in helping to establish the Christian faith in Britain and how it has withstood a series of unpredictable events during the 900 years of its existence.

Railway Notes

The railway enthusiast should not leave Kent without a visit to the world-renowned miniature Romney, Hythe & Dymchurch Railway. Built in the 1920s, the line runs for 13½ miles parallel to the shingle beaches that stretch from Dungeness to Hythe, a town close to Folkestone. The line was the brainchild of a certain Captain Howey, who in collaboration with Count Zborowski, a founder member of the Aston Martin Motor Company, developed a plan for a railway that would operate like any other but run on a 15-inch gauge track with miniature steam locomotives and carriages

Romney, Hythe & Dymchurch Railway.

to convey passengers. Ever since its inception the railway has been an outstanding success and continues to carry hundreds of passengers, including many schoolchildren, annually, providing a much needed boost to tourism in that part of Kent. In 1940 the railway was requisitioned by the Army and at one stage a miniature armoured train was developed for use should Hitler ever have decided to invade Britain.

The contrast between the eccentric notion of building a miniature steam railway and the development seventy years later of high-speed trains powered by a variety of fuel sources and designed to move people quickly and in ever greater numbers may seem incredible to those who still recall the days of the early railways. Meanwhile, we should cherish the legacy bequeathed us by our Victorian ancestors and be thankful for their vision and determination in creating the basis of a transport system not yet surpassed.

RH&DR, miniature signal box.

Train leaving Hythe.

Chapter 2

Guildford and Portsmouth

■ London's biggest terminus ■ electrification ■ **Guildford Cathedral** ■ railway maintenance
■ **Portsmouth Cathedral** ■ the cathedral of the sea ■

Getting There

Guildford is half-an-hour from Waterloo, with Portsmouth a further hour by a fast train on
the same route. There is an alternative service from Waterloo to Portsmouth via Southampton
but it takes longer than the more direct service through Guildford.

Railway Notes

Waterloo Station is the largest station in the capital and until 2007 was the London
terminus for Eurostar services to the Continent through the Channel Tunnel. From
its twenty-one platforms trains depart to serve destinations on the south coast and in
the counties of West Sussex, Hampshire and Dorset, providing both intensive commuter services
and longer-distance trains to places such as Weymouth, Exeter and Bournemouth. The pattern of
services is not dissimilar to those originally provided by the London and South Western Railway
prior to the latter's incorporation into the Southern Railway in 1927. In its heyday the Southern
Railway carried a quarter of all rail passengers in Britain and ran the largest electrification network
in the world.

South West Trains is the current service provider, using a fleet of highly efficient third rail
electric trains. The only exception is the line from Waterloo to Exeter via Salisbury, which is
not electrified. To the untutored eye one electric train looks much like another, although to the

The concourse at Waterloo Station.

The multiple track approach to Waterloo Station.

16

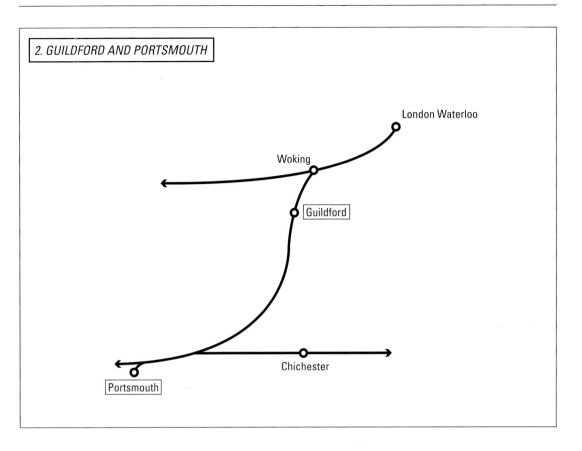

2. GUILDFORD AND PORTSMOUTH

London Waterloo

Woking

Guildford

Chichester

Portsmouth

professional railwayman all have different capabilities and characteristics that govern where and how they may be used to best effect in order to sustain one of the world's most intensively run commuter railways. Sadly, gone are the days when the public perceived trains to have character; today they all look alike, sound alike and are readily able to substitute for one another without the travelling public being aware.

Steam locomotives, which predominated for more than a hundred years until the 1960s, did possess individuality. Surprisingly, they were always referred to in the female gender. Notwithstanding, the more powerful engines regularly used on express services were given names when the assumed gender was ignored. On the East Coast line there was a class of locomotives named after famous racehorses, while the Great Western's most powerful engines were given the names of English kings and castles. As a result they became well known to the travelling public and to generations of 'railway-mad' schoolboys. While no doubt considered to be dirty and temperamental by the public, in reality they failed no more often than their modern electric and diesel counterparts and were generally less affected by weather. The performance of an electric locomotive that may use either ground-level conductor rails or overhead transmission wires to collect current may be diminished by harsh weather, when a build-up of snow and ice can lead to failure. While I would not advocate a return to the days of steam traction, many of the problems caused by the severe winter weather of 2009 and 2010 might have been minimized had steam locomotives still been in operation. No doubt there would have been other problems.

Newly constructed electrified lines are today invariably equipped with overhead wires suspended from trackside pylons for the delivery of electrical current to a locomotive. This system, which predominates in Europe, is thought to be more reliable than the original ground-level third rail collection method pioneered by the Southern Railway. However, both systems have their advantages and disadvantages, the overhead array system being particularly vulnerable to wind damage. An internal railway industry debate could be about to begin to determine whether a single system should be adopted, with third rail 'collection' being phased out and replaced. Whether the capital investment needed to convert the track can ever be procured will decide the issue. Meanwhile, third rail systems are to be found on routes radiating south from London, on Merseyside and on some Metro and underground railways; in aggregate these cover many miles of the railway network.

Guildford Cathedral

One of four cathedrals built in the twentieth century.

Look for the beautifully proportioned pillars of the nave and side aisles and the handmade kneelers throughout the cathedral.

Guildford is the largest town in Surrey but is neither the county town nor the seat of local government, which resides in Kingston-upon-Thames. In 1927 the Diocese of Guildford was created by dividing the widespread Winchester diocese into two other

The west front, Guildford Cathedral.

The nave, Guildford Cathedral.

parts, thereby creating new dioceses based upon Guildford and Portsmouth. Clearly a suitable church was needed in Guildford as a location for the bishop's seat, or *cathedra*, and the original intention was to use Holy Trinity Church in the town. However, this idea was later abandoned and in 1936 the construction of Guildford Cathedral began on Stag Hill, high above the city, on land given by the Earl of Onslow. Building progressed until 1939, when the Second World War intervened. By that stage the east end was well on the way to completion but it was not until 1961 that the cathedral was finally finished, consecration by Bishop George Reindorp taking place that year in the presence of Elizabeth II.

Sir Edward Maufe, who later planned the Air Forces Memorial at Runnymede, designed the cathedral and took a close interest in all aspects of its development, as did his wife, who made herself responsible for overseeing the embroidering of more than 1,400 kneelers, the altar cloths and canons' vestments. The period after the war was one of predictable austerity and the need to improvise resulted in a piece of an old dressing gown being incorporated into the cathedral banner. It is apparently still in use today.

The outside of the building is constructed of modern materials clad in red brick while the interior is of plaster and Doulting stone from Somerset. The plain nature of the interior design, with seven lofty nave arches that soar to the roof and the fact that there is no screen between the nave and the quire and overall little stained glass, engenders a sense of overwhelming simplicity. The building is light and airy with little adornment and this bestows a real feeling of being in a discrete place. As the cathedral guidebook says, 'Edward Maufe sought to create a building which would speak of the majesty and mystery of God and which would do so with lightness and simplicity.' The nave is one of the widest in the country.

Guildford Cathedral is dedicated to the theme of the Holy Spirit and the window at the east end depicts a dove descending. Below it is a great curtain 50 feet high that hangs behind the altar, upon which have been embroidered doves, which can also be found in many other aspects of the building. There is a regimental chapel commemorating former regiments of the county of Surrey. A chapel on the south side of the cathedral is devoted to children who have died and is used to encourage young people to visit and learn about the cathedral and its purpose. While undoubtedly not unique, it represents a firm commitment to bringing children into contact with the Church at an early age.

Guildford is one of four Anglican cathedrals completed in England in the twentieth century. Its modern style of construction may not be to everybody's taste but it represents a tangible link between the people of Surrey and the diocese of which it is the focal point. The close association between the cathedral and local people was amply demonstrated when in 1955 the Dean and Chapter launched a 'buy a brick' campaign to help to raise funds to complete their building. Their call was answered across the diocese with many individuals contributing, a brick being sold for half a crown. The idea of involving people in the financing of great projects in such a way has been successfully developed in several places since then.

Railway Notes

It is an easy hour on the train from Guildford to Portsmouth. The route threads its way through the heavily wooded hills south of Guildford to reach first Haslemere and then Petersfield, the practical limit for regular commuting to London, and thereafter across the South Downs to the coast, where it swings west towards the great city and naval base of Portsmouth.

A South West train arriving at Guildford.

When all goes smoothly a journey by train can be a convenient and enjoyable way to travel, a pleasant alternative to traffic hold-ups on the roads or frustrating delays in airport departure lounges. However, no transport system can claim to be totally trouble-free and railways have always attracted criticism for unpunctuality or lack of information, although since privatization in 1997 matters have much improved. One reason for travel disruption is the need for track maintenance and, however well managed, this can lead to temporary line closures and the use of replacement buses giving rise to longer journeys and uncertainty. Methods used to replace worn-out track and rebuild life-expired infrastructure like signalling have developed considerably in recent years, with mechanization now used whenever feasible. Gone are the days when gangs of men had physically to move track into place by hand using crowbars, or to shovel tons of ballast in order to stabilize sleepers. Even so, disruption still occurs and always will. Maintenance is an expensive business and Network Rail, the organization charged with maintaining the national network, is rightly under constant pressure to cut its costs through the adoption of new technologies.

Portsmouth Cathedral

A cathedral with close links to the Royal Navy.

Look for the twelfth-century quire, the Navy aisle and the *Golden Barque* weathervane.

Portsmouth Cathedral is rightly known as the 'cathedral of the sea' and its close connections with the Royal Navy will come as no surprise. A fifteen-minute walk from the harbour station, the cathedral lies close to the port, from where ferries depart for the Isle of Wight. The oldest part of the building goes back to 1188, when a chapel was built in honour of St Thomas of Canterbury, murdered in the reign of Henry II and canonized after his martyrdom. Only some areas of the chancel and the transepts now remain of the original church and these were damaged during the Civil War when the building, at the time being used by Royalist forces as an observation post, was shelled by Cromwell's troops stationed across the water in Gosport. The tower and nave were both virtually destroyed. On the orders of Charles II the church was rebuilt and extended after the Civil War, the work, principally involving the nave and tower, being completed by the end of the seventeenth century.

In 1927 the Diocese of Portsmouth was established and plans were made to enlarge the church to make it a building suitable for its role as the mother church of the new diocese. The former nave was to become the quire and a new nave, to be built in the 'Byzantine' style, was designed by

The west front, Portsmouth Cathedral.

The nave and organ, Portsmouth Cathedral.

Sir Charles Nicholson. Work initially began at the eastern end and by 1939 the outer shell of the new building, the tower and the transepts were all finished, as was part of the nave.

When war broke out in 1939, work was halted and did not begin again in earnest until 1983. Michael Drury was appointed as architect and by the end of 1991 his task was largely complete when the extended nave was consecrated. In 2002 the Diocese celebrated the 75th anniversary of its founding.

The cathedral marries the ancient and the modern. The nave, roomy, open and contemporary with windows of plain glass, has been joined to the quire, originally the nave of the twelfth-century church and rebuilt in 1693, while the former chancel is now the Chapel of St Thomas. The baptistry, between the nave and the quire, and beneath the tower, allows the visitor to look the length of the cathedral to the Chapel of St Thomas. The brightly decorated organ is placed between the nave and quire.

There is much of interest to see. The bishop's simple *cathedra*, a chair adjacent to the main altar in the quire, is late seventeenth-century and above it hangs the coat of arms of the diocese. Opposite the *cathedra* is the pulpit, originally built on three levels but later reduced to one. The Navy aisle on the south side contains many memorials to seafarers and officers and men of the Royal Navy. In the Chapel of Healing and Reconciliation, a window commemorating the D-Day

The *Golden Barque* weather vane.

The memorial window to Admiral Ramsay, 1939/44.

landings contains the arms of the Allied forces that took part in the Second World War and includes a memorial to Admiral Sir Bertram Ramsay, who commanded the naval forces at the time of the withdrawal from Dunkirk in 1940. He later commanded the Allied navies involved in the Normandy landings of June 1944. Close by is the grave of a member of the ship's company of the *Mary Rose*, a Tudor warship sunk off Portsmouth in 1545 and raised from the seabed more than 400 years later in 1982. In the north transept is a copy of the certificate recording the marriage of Charles II to Catherine of Braganza in 1662, while opposite is a model of the *Golden Barque*, a gilded ship and until 1954 the weather vane on the cathedral tower. The present replica on the tower is constructed of fibreglass.

The development of Portsmouth Cathedral spans several centuries from the founding of the original chapel in 1185. Its construction reflects a number of architectural periods, from the early Norman chapel to the seventeenth–century church, and thereafter to the twentieth-century extended nave with its round arches reflecting the 'Byzantine' style adopted by later architects. The building's form and ambience are so different to other cathedrals visited for this book and its many links honouring the Royal Navy, displayed in windows and memorials, so special that it should not be missed.

The tower, Portsmouth Cathedral.

Chapter 3

Chichester

The development of railways ▪ **Chichester Cathedral** ▪ the collapse of the spire in 1861
▪ Bishop George Bell ▪ modern art in the cathedral ▪ William Huskisson ▪

Getting There

Trains depart at regular intervals from Victoria Station for Portsmouth or Southampton, all of which call at Chichester. The route passes Gatwick Airport and the journey to Chichester takes approximately one-and-a-half hours.

Railway Notes

Similar to places in Kent, communities on the south coast of England have never been well served by the railway. The close proximity to the capital of several large centres of population in East and West Sussex results in journeys by train being of short duration and slow speed, planned more with the daily commuter in mind than the occasional traveller who might wish a

The opening of the London, Brighton & South Coast Railway in Sussex, 1841. (NRM)

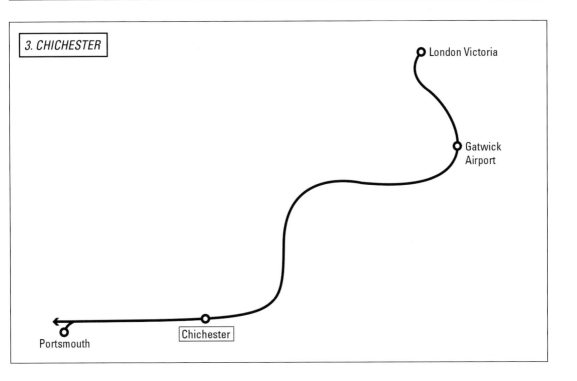

3. CHICHESTER

London Victoria

Gatwick
Airport

Portsmouth

Chichester

faster transit from one end of the line to the other. Railways in Sussex and the eastern part of Hampshire were, like routes all over the country, developed piecemeal in the nineteenth century and did not necessarily follow the most direct line between two places. Topography played a large part in determining a route but local jealousies as to which communities should benefit from a particular line, and the reverse – the wishes of some landowners not to allow the integrity of their estates to be breached by the presence of a new and intrusive system of transport – resulted in many lines taking a more torturous route than might otherwise have been necessary. Extra miles and uninspiring speeds usually resulted.

Resistance to railways was widespread in the early years of their development, with landowners frequently voicing their concerns over proposed lines and driving hard bargains to alleviate the perceived malign effects of rail transport. In seeking amelioration of such ills they demanded diversions or the hiding of tracks by the construction of tunnels and cuttings. Both the Duke of Beaufort at Badminton in Gloucestershire and his Scottish counterpart, the Duke of Atholl in Perthshire, are said to have imposed strict conditions on those railway companies that wished to pass across their land. In the case of the latter it was for many years a condition that every train should call at Blair Atholl Station lest the Duke might wish to travel.

Even in more modern times routes and train timetables are regularly adjusted and not necessarily for the convenience of the passenger. Chichester used originally to be reached from London Victoria by way of Dorking, giving a more direct route than today's trains, which now travel via Croydon and Gatwick Airport. The time difference is probably minimal but the desire of the railway companies to generate more traffic by offering additional connections and a greater number of stops, while commercially understandable, can militate against faster end-to-end services. Travel to Chichester falls into this category.

Chichester Cathedral.

Chichester Cathedral

A cathedral recently endowed with several works of contemporary art and with a free-standing bell tower.

Look for St Richard's shrine, the memorial to Bishop Bell on the Arundel Screen, the Lambert Barnard sixteenth-century paintings in the south transept and the modern works commissioned during Dean Hussey's time.

The first cathedral in Sussex was built in 681 by St Wilfrid at Selsey, 10 miles south of Chichester. The site is now under the sea. In 1075, the see or diocese of Chichester was established and a year later there began the construction of Chichester Cathedral on its present site. Started by Bishop Stigand, the work was completed in 1108 by Bishop Luffa.

Fires in 1114 and 1187 severely damaged the structure and in 1199 the cathedral was re-dedicated. In the middle of the thirteenth century the affairs of the diocese were placed in the hands of Richard of Wych and, despite his short tenure as bishop, he came to be well regarded by people and was later canonized or, as described in the cathedral guide book, 'placed in the catalogue of saints'. His shrine to the east of the high altar was destroyed in 1538 at the time of the Reformation but has since been restored to its original place in the retroquire.

The early fifteenth century saw further developments with the building of a spire, the Arundel Screen between the quire and the nave, so described because it was built by the bishop of that name, the cloisters and a bell tower. The tower is detached from the cathedral on its north side, only one of three such buildings located at an English cathedral. Meanwhile, the spire of Chichester Cathedral is 277 feet high and visible for many miles out to sea.

Disasters struck in the seventeenth century when the north-west tower collapsed and in 1642 the cathedral was damaged by Cromwell's forces when troops and their horses were billeted inside the building. Two hundred years later, the Arundel Screen was removed by the Victorians, who wished to open up the interior of the cathedral in order that they should have an uninterrupted view of what was happening in the quire. Following the removal of the screen, the spire and tower collapsed in 1861, necessitating the building of exact replicas, which were designed by Sir George Gilbert Scott.

Much controversy surrounded the collapse of the spire, which provoked considerable interest both locally and nationally. On the day in question several people witnessed the event, including a sailor who happened to be taking a bearing on the spire from his boat, while a man travelling towards Chichester by train is said to have observed the spire, glanced down at his reading material and when he next looked up, saw that it was no longer there. Another anecdote tells of a child who saw the collapse while playing in the street, ran to tell his grandfather but was scolded for his deceit until the event was confirmed, whereupon he was praised for his truthfulness!

In 1961 the Arundel Screen was restored to its original site and dedicated to the memory of Bishop George Bell, bishop of the diocese from 1929 to 1958, a tireless worker for Christian unity and a fervent opponent of Nazism and the evils visited upon the German people before and during the Second World War. He is also commemorated in Christ Church Cathedral in Oxford as described in Chapter 4 of this book. In 1984 a tapestry was commissioned to hang behind the altar in the retroquire to commemorate Bishop Bell and his work in fostering Anglo-German relations. It was designed by a German artist, Ursula Benker-Schirmer, its centrepiece being a

The nave.

Statue of William Huskisson.

The high altar and John Piper's Holy Trinity tapestry.

chalice, a symbol of St Richard. By bringing the memorials to St Richard and Bishop George Bell into one place in the cathedral, the Chichester chapter has consolidated the honour accorded to its two best-known bishops.

The south transept contains a magnificent window built in 1315. Its glass is late nineteenth-century and shows scenes from the Old and New Testaments. Also in the transept on the west wall is a large wooden panel that records the granting of land for the cathedral built at Selsey. Painted on the same panel is a picture showing Henry VIII confirming the bishopric of Robert Sherburne in the early sixteenth century while a similar panel in the north transept depicts other bishops of the diocese. All were painted by Lambert Barnard during Sherburne's time and are said to be the earliest and largest surviving contemporary Tudor portraits.

In more recent times Chichester has seen the acquisition of several examples of modern art, including John Piper's Holy Trinity tapestry, which hangs behind the high altar, Marc Chagall's window of 1978 near the east end and, in the Chapel of St Mary Magdalene, Graham Sutherland's painting *Noli me Tangere* depicting Jesus appearing to Mary on the first Easter morning. All these works were commissioned during the twenty years that Dean Hussey presided over the cathedral chapter at Chichester. Not everybody will appreciate the introduction of these modern works but, controversial or not, they certainly brighten the building. Chichester is an uncluttered and

Shrine of St Richard with the Benker-Schirmer tapestry behind.

attractive cathedral and I found it easy to navigate the interior, with information well displayed and comprehensive.

The south quire aisle contains the Romanesque Chichester Reliefs, stone carvings dating from around 1125 that tell the story of Christ's raising of Lazarus from the dead, an event that ultimately led to Christ's own crucifixion and resurrection. The carvings are unique in English architecture and have wonderfully expressive faces.

Of interest to those knowledgeable about the development of Britain's railways is a statue of William Huskisson on the north side of the nave close to the west end of the cathedral. Huskisson was for ten years member of parliament for Chichester before moving north to represent Liverpool. He was famously killed at the inauguration of the Liverpool and Manchester Railway in 1830 when he alighted from his carriage to speak to the Duke of Wellington, the prime minister of the time, and was struck by another train. He was the first man to be killed in a railway accident in Britain and there is a memorial to him adjacent to the original Liverpool to Manchester line at Rainhill. Similar details are recorded in Chapter 12 of this book describing Liverpool Cathedral.

A more recent commemoration is that of Gustav Holst, the English composer who was a close friend of Bishop George Bell. His ashes were interred in the north transept after his death in 1934, while in 2009 a plaque was erected in the wall above inscribed with the words 'the heavenly spheres make music for us' from his *Hymn of Jesus*. Holst's *Planets* suite is his best-known work and he adapted the *Jupiter* section to fit the words of Cecil Spring Rice's poem *I Vow to Thee, My Country*, turning it into the uplifting hymn so loved by many.

In the western entrance to the cathedral on either side of the main door are carved two faces; one is that of Bishop Kemp and the other of Dean Holtby, who respectively presided over the diocese and the cathedral in the latter part of the twentieth century. Such images were regularly carved in medieval times to denote figures of the times but I had not before encountered similar images from a more modern era. Since Robert Holtby retired to the Yorkshire village where I live, it gave me particular pleasure to be able to record this memorial to him.

Many will contend that the journey from Chichester to London is now no quicker than it was in the days of steam and they may well be right. Notwithstanding, the first part of the journey takes

Statue of St Richard by the north-west tower.

the traveller north through the Sussex Downs following the river Arun for much of the latter's course, past unspoilt water meadows and through heavily wooded countryside. There are striking views of Arundel Castle, the home of the Dukes of Norfolk, Earl Marshals of England for more than 500 years, and the adjoining Roman Catholic cathedral.

Chapter 4

Oxford and Winchester

■ Brunel ■ the building of the Great Western Railway ■ **Christ Church Cathedral**
■ Cardinal Wolsey's plan for a college ■ **Winchester Cathedral** ■ Alfred the Great
■ St Swithun ■ the longest nave ■ Jane Austen ■

Getting There

Oxford can be reached from London in an hour from Paddington, while the electric train service to Winchester also takes an hour from Waterloo. In addition, regular trains run directly between the two cities; these are predominantly cross-country services that link Northern England and Scotland to the south coast. Journey time between the two cities by a direct service is approximately one hour.

A visit in one day to the two cathedrals, travelling between them via Reading, and then returning from the second city directly to London is feasible although it might be best to spread your visit over two days.

Railway Notes

A name that features widely in this book is that of Isambard Kingdom Brunel, a railway pioneer of the nineteenth century who in his short life was responsible for building much of the Great Western Railway. He lived for only fifty-three years but in that time dominated railway building as an architect, civil engineer, mechanical engineer and ship designer. His achievements as one of the foremost leaders of the nineteenth-century Industrial Revolution have directly influenced the lives of all who have lived and travelled since. His is one of the most famous names in the history of engineering, if not *the* most famous, and it is little wonder that a university has now been established in his memory.

With work beginning in 1833, the Great Western Railway, or GWR, radiated west from London to eventually connect the capital with important regional centres like Birmingham, Bristol, Cardiff and Plymouth. Most of these routes to the west were surveyed by Brunel himself and laid with rails 7 feet and a ¼ inch apart – more than 2 feet wider than the gauge adopted by his competitors building lines elsewhere in the country. Details of Brunel's other achievements, particularly in the West Country, the ramifications of his choice of a wider railway gauge than that of his contemporaries and how that gauge difference was eventually reconciled are covered in Chapter 6. Suffice it to say that without Brunel's genius, determination and entrepreneurial approach much of the railway system we take for granted today would not have been built.

There was always something different about the GWR; its locomotives sported finer lines than those of other companies while, in its attitude to passengers and the marketing of services, the company generally adopted a more cultured approach than elsewhere. Its initials may have attracted the jibe that it was the 'Great Way Round' or 'God's Wonderful Railway' but people travelled in style, seemingly enjoying the experience, even if punctuality and cleanliness were

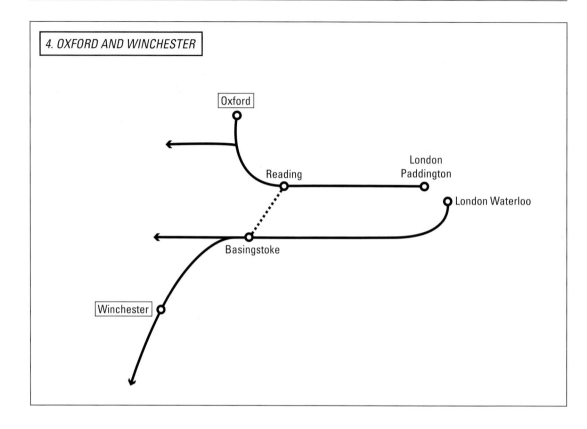

4. OXFORD AND WINCHESTER

Oxford

Reading

London Paddington

London Waterloo

Basingstoke

Winchester

not always what they might have been. To me the GWR has always been a 'railway apart'. Oxford and its nearby neighbour to the south, Didcot, where there is located a railway heritage centre, are havens of Great Western Railway memorabilia. In many places, lower quadrant semaphore signals still control train movement while the architectural style of some stations continue to reflect Brunel's grand design.

A typical GWR semaphore signal.

A cross-country express at Oxford.

The Great Western was also the first company to adopt a system of automatic train control designed to warn a train driver if he was approaching a signal set at danger and requiring him to stop. First adopted in 1908, this system proved remarkably successful and a modern version has since been developed for the whole network, thereby reducing the number of signals that might be ignored by drivers. Sadly there is now little sign of the distinctive humped ramps laid between the rails on Great Western tracks, which, when a train passed above them, triggered a cab alarm through contact with a shoe positioned beneath the locomotive. An electrically induced warning would indicate that the next signal was at danger and, if no action was taken by the driver, the brakes were applied automatically. Conversely, if the signal was clear and the train therefore authorized to continue its journey without interruption, a bell sounded in the locomotive cab. Similar principles pertain to modern control systems.

Oxford was one of the towns reached from London by the GWR and the city's present-day importance as the seat of a university and a centre for motor manufacturing mean that good communications are as essential as they were 150 years ago. The city is located on the principal freight artery from Britain's northern industrial heartlands to south coast ports, a vital route for exports.

Christt Church Cathedral

A cathedral that contains the Bishop of Oxford's *cathedra* and is also the chapel of a university college.

Look for St Frideswide's Window, the Becket Window and the Bell Altar.

Christ Church Cathedral is unlike any other in England in that it is both the seat of the Bishop of Oxford and the chapel of Christ Church College. An early church in the city was built during the lifetime of Saint Frideswide, who is celebrated as the patron saint of Oxford. She died in 727 but the location of her tomb is unknown and a shrine in her memory was destroyed during the Reformation. Some remnants were later discovered towards the end of the eighteenth century and the shrine was reconstructed at the east end of the cathedral. Frideswide's story, including her escape from the rapacious Algar, King of Leicester, who wished to abduct and marry her, is told in a window in the Latin Chapel painted in 1858 by Edward Burne-Jones, an Oxford undergraduate. Following graduation he remained at Oxford and contributed other windows in the cathedral.

The present cathedral building was constructed as a monastic church towards the end of the twelfth century to serve a community of Augustinian monks. The church was built from east to west using Cotswold stone, with its spire – said to be one of the earliest in England – being finished around 1230. There is some fine stained glass, the best probably being the Becket Window, which shows the murder of Archbishop Thomas Becket in Canterbury Cathedral in 1170. Much later, at the time of the Reformation, the martyred archbishop was condemned as a traitor and the Oxford church authorities were commanded by Henry VIII to remove any reference to him. They complied by doing the minimum, simply defacing Becket's depiction by scratching out his head from the window. Such actions were not uncommon when priests found themselves confronted by such royal edicts or the demands of zealots, who in the sixteenth and seventeenth centuries were apt to take an uncompromising line against supposed papist images or sculptures.

In 1523 Cardinal Thomas Wolsey, who became both Archbishop of York and Chancellor of England during the reign of Henry VIII, decided to found a new college at Oxford, to be called Cardinal's College. His plans for the college, which was to be built on the site of the Augustinian monastery, were grandiose and, inter alia, involved the destruction of many smaller monastic institutions to provide the necessary funds. Before the project could be completed the cardinal fell out of favour with Henry and building was halted, not being completed until towards the end of the sixteenth century. Wolsey's plans had included many alterations to Christ Church. He was one of the last medieval archbishops to be involved in the governance of his country, a role that gave him enormous power and prestige and the ear of the monarch but carried the ever-present risk of disgrace and ignominy when events took an unforeseen course. Wolsey died in 1530 on his way to London to face trial for high treason.

In 1546 the monastic church became a cathedral, one of the smallest in England. At the same time, Oxford was established as a diocese, while in 1532 Henry VIII re-founded Wolsey's college under his own name, later changing it to Christ Church. During the Civil War from 1642 to 1646, Charles I lived for a period in Oxford and worshipped in the cathedral. In the late nineteenth century much of the interior was re-designed by Sir George Gilbert Scott.

The oak Bell Altar to the north of the chancel was made in 2000 and is dedicated to the memory of Bishop George Bell, who studied at Christ Church and later became Bishop of Chichester. A close friend of Dietrich Bonhoeffer, one of the leaders of the anti-Nazi German Confessional Church, Bishop Bell bravely opposed the saturation bombing of German cities in the Second World War. His celebrated words are recorded on the altar: 'No nation, no church, no individual is guiltless. Without repentance and without forgiveness there can be no regeneration.' Chapter 3 contains references to Bell's episcopacy at Chichester.

The onward journey from Oxford to Winchester is straightforward and takes little more than an hour. After Reading, an important Great Western Railway town and strategic junction currently being re-modelled to enable it to handle increased traffic, cross-country services move onto the lines of the former Southern Railway leading directly to Winchester and the south coast.

Winchester Cathedral

The cathedral was begun in 1079 when Winchester was the capital city of England.

Look for the nave (the longest in England), the chantry chapels, the diver's memorial and Jane Austen's brass tablet on the wall of a side aisle.

The Bishop of Winchester is the fifth most senior bishop in the Church of England and one of twenty-six Lords Spiritual who sit as ex officio members of the House of Lords. It is appropriate that his cathedral should be a fine church inspiring great loyalty and appreciation from the people of Hampshire. At its inception the diocese covered a much greater area than it does today, but growing populations led to the creation of new dioceses centred upon Guildford and Portsmouth in the twentieth century.

The first Winchester Cathedral was a Saxon church started in about 648. It soon became the cathedral church of the diocese and an important royal and ecclesiastical centre. Alfred the Great, whose statue stands at the eastern entrance to the city, was King of Wessex and was buried in the cathedral when he died in 899. In the next century, that cathedral was rebuilt as part of a Benedictine priory and was dedicated to St Swithun, a ninth-century saint. Legend has it that when Swithun died in 862, he requested that his remains be buried in the cathedral churchyard, where the rain would fall upon them. When in 971 he was reburied inside the cathedral it is alleged that he was so angry that he made it rain for forty days. St Swithun's day falls on 15 July and that day has long been associated with the likelihood of a period of prolonged wet weather should the day be inclement. A modern memorial to St Swithun stands in the retroquire, replacing one that was destroyed on the orders of Henry VIII in 1538.

Following the demolition of the Saxon building in 1093 the present cathedral was developed by Bishop William Wakelin. Thereafter his Norman cathedral was added to by successive bishops as and when resources became available and ideas emerged. The nave and west end were radically transformed by William of Wykeham, also the founder of New College at Oxford and Winchester College, when he served as bishop between 1367 and 1404. Much later changes came in the early years of the twentieth century when the cathedral was restored by work undertaken by T.G. Jackson. It was during this time that William Walker, a professional diver, embarked upon extensive work to shore up the south and east walls of the cathedral using more than a million bricks and concrete blocks and 25,000 tons of cement. Working in total darkness at depths of up to 20 feet, he repacked the waterlogged foundations, thereby forestalling almost certain collapse. There is a memorial to Walker, complete with his diver's helmet, on the south side of the Lady chapel.

Winchester Cathedral, the north side showing the length of the nave.

The west front.

The magnificence of the Perpendicular nave is Winchester's crowning glory. At a length of 535 feet it is one of the longest naves in any Gothic cathedral in England and makes an immediate impression on the visitor entering the building from the west end. Medieval cathedrals and abbeys tended to be built with very long side aisles and naves in order to accommodate the liturgical processions that were such a feature of early worship. Other cathedrals with very long naves include those at Ely, Peterborough and St Albans. Work ordered by Bishop William of Wykeham led to the remodelling of the nave, the height and vaulting of which instil a sensation of great dignity.

The two transepts, however, remain in their original Romanesque form. Throughout the cathedral there are a number of chantry chapels containing the tombs of former bishops, where in medieval times masses were said or sung for the souls of the departed. Chantries were at one time built in many cathedrals and churches to honour the dead but many have since been removed. However, at Winchester the chantry chapel of William of Wykeham remains in its original position on the south side of the nave, with his effigy intact.

The Norman tower collapsed in 1107 and was rebuilt starting in 1202. Its squat appearance is as distinctive a feature of Winchester as is the Great Screen behind the high altar. Constructed in the late fifteenth century during the time when William Waynflete was bishop, the screen was originally carved with figures from the Old Testament, prophets and saints and some of the cathedral's benefactors. During the Reformation many of these were removed on the orders of Henry VIII, since when new sculptures have been installed.

The nave.

Many are the famous names associated with Winchester. William II was buried under the tower in 1100 following his death in a hunting accident in the nearby New Forest. Henry IV was married there, as were Queen Mary and Philip of Spain in 1554, while other royal personages were baptised in the cathedral. At the time of the Civil War Cromwell's troops plundered the cathedral and carried away many of its books and other treasures. More recently, in 1817 Jane Austen was buried in the north nave aisle following her death in Winchester shortly after she had travelled there from her home at Chawton, to the east of the city. She is remembered for her great literary works such as *Sense and Sensibility* and *Pride and Prejudice* and her grave attracts many visitors. So much so that one cathedral verger was once heard to remark that 'there's something special about that lady.' There is a memorial to her on the north side of the nave.

Winchester has for centuries stood at a junction of many routes. It is as easily reached today as it was in Norman times when for 200 years it was the capital of England, sharing that privilege with London. Almost every period since the early twelfth century is represented in the city's architecture. Its magnificent Norman cathedral, which took 300 years to build, dominates the city and probably contains more history than any equivalent place. Its connections with monarchs and princes down the centuries are more numerous than anywhere outside London. Over the years it has been visited by many thousands of pilgrims travelling the Pilgrim's Way, originally created to link Canterbury and Winchester. Today the city remains an important administrative centre, easily accessible by train, and a place that should certainly be seen.

Gary Price, Clerk of the Works at Salisbury Cathedral, at the top of the spire. (Salisbury Cathedral)

Chapter 5

Salisbury

■ Early railway competition ■ **Salisbury Cathedral** ■ the tallest spire
■ the chapter house ■ the *Magna Carta* ■

Getting There

The journey from Waterloo to Salisbury takes approximately two hours using the Exeter service. However, some trains terminate at Salisbury.

Railway Notes

The majority of trains that start their journeys from the six former Southern Railway terminuses in London provide short duration services, principally for those commuting to work in the City or day visitors to the capital. Most of these routes were electrified during the twentieth century to improve their efficiency. However, one exception was the route from Waterloo to Salisbury and Exeter, one of the Southern Railway's few long-distance main lines, which, despite political pressure for its conversion to electrical traction, continues to use diesel haulage.

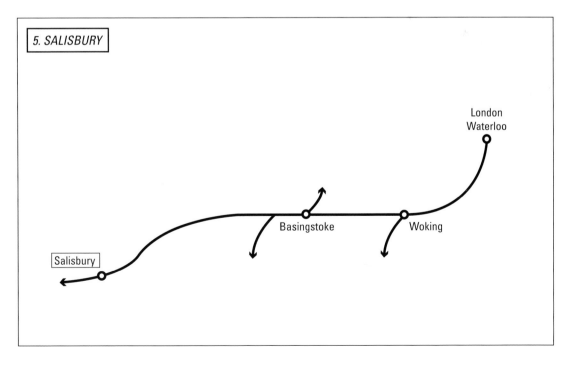

5. SALISBURY

London
Waterloo

Basingstoke

Woking

Salisbury

Prior to the nationalization of the country's four main railway companies in 1947, the Southern and Great Western companies competed for traffic to the West of England. Their routes were broadly similar in length and each set out to capitalize on the holiday market, which started to grow after the First World War as Britain's population took advantage of the increasing mobility conferred by railways. Both companies served Exeter from London and from there the Great Western connected to Torquay and Cornwall while the Southern established routes to Barnstaple in North Devon and Bude on the North Cornish coast. The competition could be intense, the more so since at Exeter, Southern trains had to use the Great Western–owned St David's Station and its tracks for a short distance to access its own route to North Devon. This was not an uncommon occurrence at the time since, as described in Chapter 3, railway development in the nineteenth century tended to be unsystematic, leading to anomalies that could only be resolved by later agreement to share the network. Negotiations were never easy as commercial interests were involved and could become very bitter especially if, as sometimes occurred, the host company deliberately delayed the trains of a rival compelled to use its tracks.

After nationalization in 1947, railways declined in importance. Chapter 16 describes some of the measures taken to reduce the size of the network in the belief that the motor car would in future provide the most convenient and economic means of personal transport over short to medium distances. Fifty years later, frustrations experienced when travelling by air, the growing costs of motoring and a realization that sources of fossil fuels are finite, have all led to a general renaissance in rail travel. The service from London to Salisbury is a route that has benefitted from this change of attitude as passenger numbers have increased. Meanwhile, a provision of the 1997 legislation establishing greater freedoms for train operators was that competition should be permitted and encouraged where demand and routes made it feasible. While companies like Hull Trains and Grand Central are amongst those to successfully challenge larger operators, others have had less success in providing financially sustainable alternative services.

Salisbury Cathedral

The cathedral with the tallest spire in England.

Look for the world's oldest working clock in the nave, the Morning Chapel and the memorial to Rex Whistler, the chapter house and Salisbury's copy of the *Magna Carta*.

The Salisbury area is steeped in history and long before the Romans came to Britain, Iron Age settlements had been created across the surrounding countryside of Salisbury Plain. The best known of these ancient settlements was built at Stonehenge, although there is considerable dispute as to when and how the stone circle there first came to be established and for what purpose. Pamela Street's book *Portrait of Wiltshire* gives some clues to how Stonehenge may have come into existence.

At Sarum a few miles south of Stonehenge there was an Iron Age camp that the Romans and later the Normans developed into a bigger settlement, the latter building both a royal castle and a cathedral, the ground plan of which can still be seen. Sarum lies just to the north of present-day Salisbury. At the end of the twelfth century Bishop Herbert Poore decided that the site was too small for all those who wished to occupy it and determined that a new cathedral should be built

The west front, Salisbury Cathedral.

on the water meadows adjacent to the nearby river Avon. The community that grew up around the bishop's chosen location was named New Sarum, or Salisbury.

Herbert Poore died before his ideas for the new cathedral could be realized. However, he was succeeded as bishop by his brother, Richard Poore, who in 1220 began the work of implementing his sibling's plans for a replacement for the Old Sarum cathedral. This task was completed in the remarkably short time of thirty-eight years. As a result Salisbury Cathedral is built largely in a single style, that of the Early English Gothic period, unlike many other medieval cathedrals where construction took many decades and crossed the boundaries from one architectural period to another. Locally quarried limestone was used in the cathedral's construction.

A principal feature of Salisbury Cathedral and the one most likely to catch the eye of a visitor is its elegant tower and spire rising to a height of 404 feet, the tallest of any church in England. Begun later than the rest of the cathedral but completed by 1320, the tower and spire replaced an earlier lantern tower, adding 6,500 tons to the weight of the original structure. An internal wooden framework was constructed to assist the building of the spire and it is still in place. To allow external inspections of the spire a series of iron rungs have been inserted into the masonry, enabling a man to climb right to the top.

I visited Salisbury early on a bright spring morning, possibly the best time to see the cathedral, which was almost deserted at the time. The nave is built in the style of the period and provides plenty of space for the major services held there. On the north side is situated the oldest working clock in the world, built in 1386 and until 1789 housed in a detached bell tower; the clock has no

The quire and high altar with the Trinity Chapel beyond.

face and only strikes the hour. In the centre of the nave is a new font designed by William Pye and consecrated in 2008 by Archbishop Rowan Williams of Canterbury on the occasion that the cathedral celebrated 750 years. The sign of the cross made by the archbishop on the four sides of the font are clearly visible.

Two very different people connected with the early years of the cathedral are commemorated within its precincts. William Longespee, whose tomb stands on the south side of the nave, was present when the foundations were built and was subsequently the first person to be buried there. He was King John's half-brother and was instrumental in helping to persuade the monarch to agree terms prescribed by the barons when the *Magna Carta* was drawn up and signed at Runnymede in June 1215. The other, Elias of Dereham in Norfolk, was at one stage a canon of Salisbury and is thought to have been closely involved in the building of the cathedral. He was also involved in the preparation of the *Magna Carta*.

Moving eastwards up the nave the visitor comes to the central crossing. Standing in the centre of the crossing you can clearly identify the extent to which the supporting pillars have over time bent under the additional weight of the tower and spire. To help to distribute this weight, buttresses and bracing arches were incorporated at the time of building, with more work being carried out at various times since to provide even greater stability. The structure of the tower and the spire has also been reinforced by the use of iron ties and brackets and, as recently as the late 1980s, both underwent considerable renovation. Today the spire leans approximately 30 inches out of true towards the south-west but is reported to have shown little or no movement in recent years.

When originally built the entrance to the quire was hidden by a screen, or *pulpitum*, but this was removed during extensive restoration work in 1790. A section of the screen was then incorporated into the Morning Chapel, so named because it was probably where the first service of the day was held in medieval times. In one corner of the Morning Chapel is a memorial to Rex Whistler, the artist, killed in action during the Second World War in Normandy in 1944 following the Allied invasion of Europe. He lived in the nearby cathedral close and the memorial, a revolving glass prism engraved by his brother Laurence, depicts the cathedral.

Some of the stalls in the quire have intricately carved misericords beneath the 'tip-up' seats and date from 1236. The backs of some of the stalls indicate the names of the ancient prebends, or parish estates, which in earlier times belonged to the Church and provided support for the clergy. Others show the name of a cathedral office holder such as the dean or the precentor. A member of the cathedral staff whom I encountered while in the quire told me that what she most enjoyed about the cathedral were the feelings of unity and tradition that working within its precincts inspired: 'unity', she explained, because it was built over such a short period of time and therefore reflected a single architectural period, and 'tradition' because services in Salisbury still reflected more established forms of Anglican worship.

At the east end is the Trinity Chapel, the earliest part of the cathedral, finished in 1225, with its roof supported by narrow pillars of Purbeck marble. The cathedral guide book comments

The medieval clock dating from about 1386.

The nave looking west.

that 'the shafts of marble must have been a source of wonder to people used to the massive, solid columns of the Norman cathedral at Old Sarum,' from where Bishop Poore had moved the cathedral community only a few years previously. The east window of the chapel, a mixture of blue and red colours, is dedicated to people persecuted for their beliefs. It was made by Gabriel Loire at Chartres in France towards the end of the twentieth century and has as its centrepiece Christ dying on the cross.

For me one of the most interesting discoveries in the cathedral was that of the Altar of St Margaret of Scotland in the south transept. Margaret was the wife of Malcolm III, King of Scotland, and was a great influence on the Celtic Church, in her time bringing it more into line with the practices of the Church of Rome. She was a descendant of Alfred the Great and was canonized in 1250. My own church in Yorkshire is a rare dedication to St Margaret but why she should feature so prominently in Salisbury Cathedral is a mystery. As I later discovered, Margaret is also commemorated in Durham Cathedral; the link between that cathedral and Salisbury is mentioned in Chapter 15.

The chapter house, the traditional meeting place of the clergy, is reached by walking through the cloisters. A wonderfully bright octagonal building with a beautifully worked fan-vaulted roof supported by a central column, the chapter house contains a thirteenth-century frieze that runs around the inside of the building just above head height. It depicts scenes from the books of Genesis and Exodus and shows in easily understandable form some of the best-known biblical stories of the Old Testament; the expulsion of Adam and Eve from the Garden of Eden, Noah's Ark, the intended sacrifice of Isaac by Abraham and countless other scenes are all easily identified with the aid of an explanatory leaflet.

However, the central feature of the chapter house is the exhibition of Salisbury Cathedral's copy of the *Magna Carta* of 1215. One of only four original copies, the others being in the British Library or at Lincoln, the *Magna Carta* is written in Latin on calfskin. The scribe was Elias of Dereham, already mentioned, who, once King John and his nobles had agreed the terms of their accord, was given the task of squeezing 3,500 words of the detail onto vellum. The *Magna Carta's* principal effect was to safeguard the freedoms of the Church, to enshrine the privileges of the barons and to restrict abuses of royal power. Provisions in the treaty were subsequently incorporated into the English Bill of Rights of 1689. Later still, many of its stipulations were included in drafts of both the American Declaration of Independence of 1776 and the Declaration of Human Rights by the General Assembly of the United Nations in 1948. *See also* Chapter 9 for Hereford Cathedral's connection with *Magna Carta*.

To the west of the chapter house are the cathedral cloisters, the largest in England and completed in 1266. Salisbury was never a monastic foundation and so the cloisters must have been designated for the use of the canons or for other purposes relevant to the cathedral. They provide a fitting area through which to depart this most gracious of churches, which towers above the city clustered around it – proof, should proof be needed, of the dedication and ingenuity of its Norman builders and the foresight of the Church's early bishops.

South West

Exeter Cathedral.

Chapter 6

Exeter and Truro

■ Named trains ■ **Exeter Cathedral** ■ Brunel's railway to the West
■ the Royal Albert Bridge ■ **Truro Cathedral** ■

Getting There

Exeter can be reached by one of two parallel routes, either from Paddington in two-and-a-quarter hours or from Waterloo in three-and-a-half hours. The latter service, while longer in time is often less crowded, particularly in the busy holiday months of July and August. Both routes serve St David's Station in Exeter.

The onward journey to Truro from Exeter takes two-and-a-half hours.

Railway Notes

At the beginning of the twentieth century railway companies sought various ways to publicize their train services and capitalize upon the notion that travel by rail, however slow or tedious, was an exciting adventure to be undertaken as much for its enjoyment as for the means of reaching a destination. Seaside resorts, the Lake District or the Western Isles were all portrayed in brightly painted posters, many of them featuring jolly fishermen or happy

Brunel's Royal Albert Bridge at Saltash.

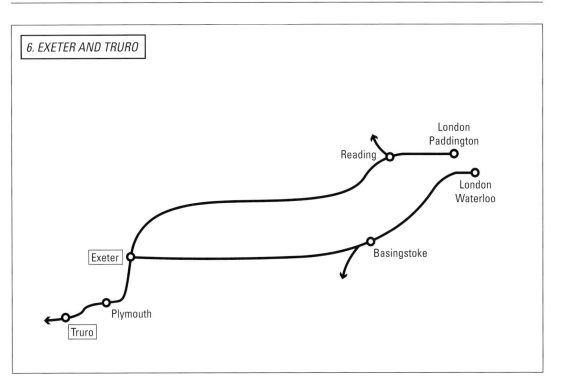

London
Paddington

Reading

London
Waterloo

Exeter

Basingstoke

Plymouth

Truro

A local train for Falmouth departs Truro.

holidaymakers. As an advertising ploy such material no doubt had its advantages and today similar publicity is still used, although usually more restrained in tone.

In pursuit of other means of publicizing destinations and routes, the 'big four' companies also named their more prestigious trains, highlighting increasing speeds and the convenience conferred by, for example, restaurant and sleeping cars. Some sleeper trains still exist today and would seem to have a reasonably assured future. On the other hand, restaurant cars, despite a revival on certain routes following privatization in 1997, are now generally being replaced by buffet cars and the ubiquitous snack trolley. Only a few train companies still offer a dining service and there is little prospect that even they will necessarily survive for long.

However, some modern expresses are still proclaimed by name, their titles having endured in one form or another for more than a hundred years. The *Flying Scotsman* to Edinburgh from King's Cross and the *Cornish Riviera Express* from Paddington to Cornwall both remain in today's timetable. Other named trains like the *Northern Irishman* or the *Royal Highlander*, the overnight train to Inverness from London, have sadly disappeared and with them has gone some of the fascination and romance of rail travel.

Exeter Cathedral

Devon's glorious twelfth-century cathedral.

Look out for the view from the quire towards the east end, the minstrel's gallery above the nave, Bishop Bronscombe's tomb, the Exeter Clock in the north tower and below it the door that has a hole at its base to allow a small animal to pass.

Exeter, on the main railway to Cornwall, is a large city and an important regional centre, being the seat of local government in Devon and the focus for many of the county's commercial and municipal services. Exeter Cathedral stands in the centre of the city, the mother church of a diocese that once encompassed all of Devon and Cornwall; the bishop's seat was originally located in a large church at Crediton, 7 miles to the north, from where it was moved to Exeter in 1050. Today one of the two suffragans, or deputy bishops, appointed to assist the Bishop of Exeter in the administration of the diocese has the title of Bishop of Crediton. However, he has no cathedral of his own.

Built in the Norman style the present cathedral was started in 1114 and completed by 1180. A particular aspect of that building was the inclusion of twin towers flanking the cathedral to the north and south. These were built by William Warelwast, a nephew of William the Conqueror, who had been appointed bishop by his uncle in 1107. Just less than a hundred years later, plans were set in hand to rebuild the Norman cathedral in the Decorated Gothic style and the twin towers were incorporated as the north and south transepts of the new building, where they stand like massive castle keeps flanking the nave, an arrangement said to be unique amongst English medieval cathedrals. These and other changes proceeded under the direction of four very gifted bishops until 1369, since when the cathedral has remained largely unaltered.

The nave of the cathedral is one of the widest in England and was finished by Bishop John Grandisson in the fourteenth century. Supported by Purbeck marble pillars and with no central tower, the magnificent roof vaulting stretches from one end of the cathedral to the other, the

Exeter Cathedral; the north side and St Paul's Tower.

longest continuous extent of medieval vaulting in the world. Because the screen, or *pulpitum*, is no longer a solid wall dividing the nave from the quire it is possible to stand towards the west end of the cathedral and look past the screen to the quire and high altar beyond, something not feasible in many other medieval cathedrals. Placed in the centre of the screen is the massive cathedral organ, originally built in 1665.

On the north side of the nave high up in the triforium is a minstrel gallery carved with angels playing fourteenth-century instruments, with behind it a room that acts as an echo chamber. The gallery is still used on special occasions. Also at ground level on the same side of the nave is a memorial to the Bengal Lancers, a regiment also known as the Delhi Spearmen for its expertise with the lance when capturing the city of that name during the 1857 Indian Mutiny. The Lancers later set sail from Calcutta in 1859, returning to Exeter having won fourteen Victoria Crosses during their time in India. Meanwhile, the roof of the nave is studded with bosses weighing up to 2 tons; some have been repainted recently in bright colours, making it easier to identify what they represent. A boss depicting the murder of St Thomas Becket by Henry II's knights in Canterbury Cathedral is easily identified towards the west end.

As already noted, the screen allows a more or less uninterrupted view of the quire, it having been opened up by Sir George Gilbert Scott when he undertook certain reconstruction work in the cathedral in the 1870s. There is a woodcarving of the crucifixion of Christ beneath the

The Lady chapel.

screen's north side that depicts in graphic detail what the carver sensed must have been the chaotic scenes around the cross during Christ's agony. It is thought to have originated from The Netherlands around 1500 and is on loan.

The north transept, which from the inside gives no clue to the fact that it is one of the cathedral's former Norman towers, houses the Exeter Clock, placed there in 1484. Below the clock is a wooden door, at the base of which is a hole big enough to allow a small animal to pass through. Created many decades ago, this allowed the bishop's cat to enter the transept to control vermin, which were no doubt rife in those days. Mice were particularly attracted to the clock's mechanism, which was greased with fat; their behaviour in running up the clock's ropes in their search for food is thought to have given rise to the words of that age-old nursery rhyme *Hickory, dickory, dock, the mouse ran up the clock … .*

Exeter was bombed on several occasions in the early summer of 1942. Following Allied aerial attacks on the ancient German cities of Lubeck and Cologne, Hitler vowed to take revenge on any city in Britain that merited a three-star rating in the *Baedeker Travel Guide*. Bath, York, Norwich and Exeter, and later Canterbury, were all cities targeted by the Luftwaffe. During May and the first week of June that year, Exeter was hit on a number of occasions, resulting in several deaths and damage to the cathedral and other buildings. The Chapel of St James was totally destroyed

The minstrel's gallery above the nave.

on the night of 4 May. Elsewhere, windows were blown out and the fabric of the Lady chapel and south quire aisle was damaged, the latter not being repaired until after hostilities ended in 1945. Whilst Canterbury and York were bombed, neither Canterbury Cathedral nor York Minster were hit, although some important historic buildings in both cities were damaged.

Exeter Cathedral has a large and fine collection of tombs and memorials. Many commemorate the lives of former bishops who contributed so much to enhancing the cathedral in the fourteenth century. The cathedral guide book makes special mention of the tomb of Bishop Walter Bronscombe near the Lady chapel. He died in 1280 and his effigy is recorded as being amongst the finest, dressed as he is in his bishop's robes, 'with two angels, carrying his shield, looking upwards expectantly, so that the figure seems ready for life rather than death.'

The Lady chapel was the first part of the cathedral to be restructured in the fourteenth century. Following the damage sustained during the Second World War many of the windows were replaced with clear glass, with the exception of the East Window, which is painted. Indeed, Exeter Cathedral is brightly illuminated by natural light, the presence of a large number of clear glass windows contributing to this effect.

The quire, with its towering fourteenth-century bishop's throne, or *cathedra*, complete with its magnificent carved elephant misericord, and the even older quire stalls, was much damaged at the

The hole that allowed the passage of a cat.

The Great West Window.

time of the Reformation and it was not until the nineteenth century that restoration work took place under the auspices of George Gilbert Scott, who was commissioned to return the area to its former glory. For visitors this must be the loveliest part of the cathedral as they look east towards the high altar, then through the two arches immediately behind to see the Lady chapel beyond, before finally looking upwards to observe the Great East Window above them. The Great East Window contains figures of Abraham, Moses and Isaiah dating from 1304 and a central depiction of Mary with the baby Jesus, surrounded by saints.

William of Orange arrived in Britain in 1688, landing at Torbay, and stopped in Exeter for a period before marching to London, where he later ousted James II from the throne. He is said to have contemplated his next moves while occupying the bishop's throne in Exeter Cathedral, moves that must subsequently have heartened those Protestants who wished to see the back of the Catholic James. Equally they must have dismayed others who had by then grown tired of the seemingly endless conflict over what form of Christian worship should be followed in Britain, a debate that occupied peoples' minds during much of the reigns of the Tudor and Stuart monarchs.

There is much else to see in the cathedral and it is a joy to wander around such an interesting and inspiring building. The medieval chapter house and the library, where a visitor can see displayed the *Exeter Book*, meticulously written in the eleventh century and presented by Edward the Confessor in 1050, should be visited. Also on display is the *Exeter Domesday*, which records a survey of land holdings in South West England even before similar work ordered by William the Conqueror after 1066. The area on the south side of the cathedral is the site of the original cloisters, where in the nineteenth century John Loughborough Pearson, the architect of Truro Cathedral, devised a scheme to replicate a section of them.

Railway Notes

The line westwards from Exeter into Cornwall is one of the most picturesque routes in Britain and, for the railway enthusiast, one of great interest. Its construction faced those who built it, most notably Isambard Kingdom Brunel, with some formidable challenges. As a railway pioneer Brunel was responsible for laying out much of the Great Western Railway, initially built to a gauge between the rails of 7 feet and a ¼ inch. His justification for such a gauge was that it would be safer and permit higher speeds. However, his competitors elsewhere had adopted a gauge of 4 feet, 8½ inches and in 1892 it was decided that all broad-gauge lines should be converted so that a standard template could be established across the country. Brunel died in 1859 at the comparatively early age of fifty-three, having in his short life been responsible for the construction of more than 1,200 miles of railway in England and Wales, much of it still in use today. He also built some of the first iron-clad steamships, the Rotherhithe and Box tunnels, the Royal Albert Bridge at Saltash and Paddington Station, and also involved himself in the construction of some overseas railways. *See also* Chapter 4.

West of Exeter the railway hugs the coast before turning inland to cross the southern slopes of Dartmoor. Some sections of line close to the sea can be disrupted by storms, with waves often breaking over the rails, leading to the temporary suspension of train services. This situation has existed ever since the line was built in the 1840s and a number of solutions have been advanced to overcome the problem, one being that the original Southern Railway route from Exeter to Plymouth should be used instead; unfortunately, Dr Beeching put paid to that alternative when he recommended closure of the route in the 1960s.

The route beyond Newton Abbot towards Plymouth necessitates trains climbing three major inclines at Dainton, Rattery and Hemerdon, close to the South Devon villages of those names. While none are of significant height each bank is steep and in the days of steam haulage they imposed considerable demands on a locomotive and its crew. A temporary signal check, damp weather causing driving wheels to slip or the failure of an engine to steam freely

Isambard Kingdom Brunel, as painted by his brother-in-law, J.C. Horsley, in 1833. (Brunel Engine House)

resulting in poor performance, could all lead to a heavy train stalling and falling behind schedule. From the outset Brunel and other Victorian engineers had their doubts as to the ability of steam locomotives to move heavy loads over such a steep route and Brunel at one stage devised an experimental atmospheric railway that involved the use of air pressure to assist trains. While the system worked under ideal conditions, the equipment proved vulnerable to external influences, including rats eating the leather membrane sealing the pressure tubes, and had eventually to be abandoned, a rare but costly failure. Today diesel locomotives generally cope well with this difficult piece of railway.

After leaving Plymouth the railway enters Cornwall, crossing the river Tamar at Saltash, the site of one of Brunel's greatest engineering triumphs. It is here that trains pass over the river by the high-level Royal Albert Bridge. Opened in 1859, five months before Brunel's death, the bridge comprises two main spans each 455 feet in length, braced by two huge cylindrical top tubes with decking held rigidly in place by cross-bracing chains. The bridge took more than three years to build. Technically it is a 'closed' suspension bridge, the stresses all being absorbed within the structure itself. The bridge carries a single railway track and since 1969 has been duplicated by a separate but parallel road bridge to the north.

Many of the still working railways in Cornwall originated as mineral lines to transport tin and later china clay to local ports. The piecemeal construction of these lines began to be rationalized at the beginning of the twentieth century when the Great Western Railway gradually bought up those that remained. Eventually the company controlled all the principal routes that today comprise the main line from Plymouth to Penzance, with branches to towns like Newquay and Falmouth. Much of the present-day traffic constitutes the carriage of holidaymakers, although there are still some residual freight workings.

Cornwall's railways have their own character. The Great Western culture runs deep and stations, signal boxes, name boards and semaphore signals all reflect the old order, although the main line has been considerably improved in recent years. The route follows a torturous course above the many inlets that penetrate the southern coast of the county, necessitating the construction of several viaducts and numerous tunnels, many built by Brunel. Approximately an hour after crossing the Tamar the line reaches Truro, the only city in Cornwall and the administrative centre of the county.

Truro Cathedral

A cathedral since 1910 and the mother church of the Cornish Diocese.

Look for the three rose windows, the *Way of the Cross* terracotta frieze and John Miller's painting, *Cornubia, Land of the Saints*.

Truro Cathedral was completed in 1910 and was at the time the only new Anglican cathedral to have been built since the Reformation. Designed by John Loughborough Pearson, mentioned earlier in this chapter for his work on the Exeter cloisters, in a revival of the Early English style, the cathedral is set in the bustling heart of the city, closely surrounded by buildings, and in that respect not unlike Newcastle Cathedral with its limited surrounding precincts. It is built upon the site of the former St Mary's Church.

Truro Cathedral from the south.

The *Way of the Cross* frieze.

The quire and nave.

A Cornish diocese was re-established in 1877 following 800 years when the affairs of the Church in the West Country had been directed from Exeter. Their wish to have their own diocese finally met, the aspirations of the Cornish people were that its mother church should be based within the county; Bodmin was a candidate for the site of the cathedral, as was the ancient parish of St Germans near Saltash, but the prize went to Truro. Bishop Benson, who later became Archbishop of Canterbury, was appointed as the first bishop and it was due to his leadership and energy that the new cathedral was completed in such a relatively short time. He presided over the new diocese and the building of its cathedral for five short years before being summoned to Canterbury, his achievements in those years as much as others accomplish in a lifetime.

Pearson, who designed a number of churches during his lifetime, which covered the period of Gothic Revival in church building, died while Truro Cathedral was still in the early stages of construction. It was left to his son, Frank Pearson, to complete his father's work.

The cathedral is one of the few Anglican cathedrals to have been built with three spires. Inside the visitor gets an uninterrupted view the whole length of the building, since there is no quire screen, and this bestows an impression of simple dignity. Everything about the cathedral gives the visitor a feeling of being in a special place, which, while only a hundred years old, seeks to emulate its older medieval counterparts in proclaiming its faith in Christ.

Cornubia, Land of the Saints.

There are three rose windows; that in the north transept symbolizing the root of Jesse, the window in the south transept, Pentecost, and the third at the west end, the Creation. In total there are more than seventy windows, all designed and made by Victorian craftsmen. The Great East Window depicts the Last Judgement, showing Christ in victory over death.

Local Cornish features were not forgotten when the glass was planned. The Fishermen's Window in the Boer War Chapel celebrates sea fishing while there is a depiction of the mining industry in the Chapel of Unity and Peace. Both these industries have suffered severe decline in recent years.

On the north side of the cathedral near the quire is a clay sculpture showing the Way of the Cross. Designed and constructed by George Tinworth, a sculptor working for the china firm Doultons, it shows the road to Calvary with Christ carrying his cross and Simon of Cyrene being persuaded to assist him. The crowd scenes that form a backcloth to the central drama of the sculpture create a real feeling of the passions that ran so high on the occasion; the fearful glances of the Roman soldiers, rabble-rousers in the crowd, the deep concerns of the women watching events unfold and Christ himself, calm, placating those gripped by hysteria and resigned to his fate. All are shown in this most moving tableau. The sculpture was given by Mr F.W. Bond in gratitude for the safe return of his two sons from the Boer War.

A London-bound express approaching Truro.

Cornwall has always been a place apart and its mysterious past is exemplified by a painting in the cathedral called *Cornubia, Land of the Saints*. It gives an overview of the county and the diocese – the two are almost co-terminus, although included are two parishes in Devon – with crosses denoting the position of each parish and showing places dedicated to Celtic saints. The earliest Celtic Christian roots in Britain were established west of the river Tamar and the use of ancient saints' names in the dedication of churches underlines the historical importance of the area. Quoting an old Cornish saying, the cathedral guidebook puts it that 'there are more saints in Cornwall than there are in heaven'. It is not hard to understand why the Cornish campaigned for so long to restore their diocese and build a cathedral of their own in the late nineteenth century.

I visited Truro Cathedral early on a bright Saturday morning in July. The absence of other visitors, the skilful work of the volunteer flower arrangers and the organist's rehearsal of the following day's hymns all combined to bestow a great feeling of serenity and dedication. I left feeling that Cornwall's cathedral was in good hands.

A High Speed Train for Paddington at Truro.

Chapter 7

Wells

Getting There

Wells is no longer connected to the railway network and the nearest mainline station is Castle Cary situated on the route from Paddington to the West of England. Travel time from Paddington is approximately an hour-and-a-half and a taxi or a bus should be used to complete the 12-mile journey to Wells.

An alternative route from London would be to take a train from Paddington to Bristol or Bath, both stations being served by fast trains from the capital. Again a bus or taxi should be used for the connection to Wells.

Railway Notes

Wells was never on a main railway route and the branch lines that once served it were mostly closed either prior to or following the Beeching review of the 1960s. Indeed at one time Wells had three stations connecting it to other towns in the county, giving links to more distant destinations. Today North Somerset is ill-provided with rail transport and those routes that still exist generally connect to London or Bristol with little local provision.

However, prior to its closure by Beeching there was a through route that linked Bath with Bournemouth on the South Coast, a rural line, slow and often unreliable. That line justified itself principally by the number of holidaymakers it carried every summer from Lancashire and the Midlands to South Coast seaside resorts. The Somerset & Dorset Railway, or the 'S&D' as it was fondly known, originated in the Somerset Central Railway, which connected Glastonbury

A GWR locomotive on the West Somerset heritage railway.

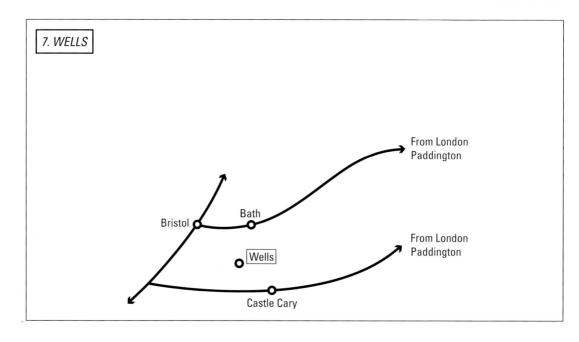

7. WELLS

From London
Paddington

Bristol

Bath

Wells

From London
Paddington

Castle Cary

Inside the cab of a former GWR locomotive on the WSR.

to the main line between Bristol and Exeter and to the ports situated on the southern shores of the Bristol Channel. This line was built in 1854 and Wells was connected to it by a branch five years later. Route rationalization soon took place and following the purchase of some smaller uneconomic lines in the area by their larger neighbours, through routes connecting important regional centres were eventually established. The S&D was created in this way.

The S&D was jointly operated by the Midland Railway and the London & South Western Railway until 1923 when, following the Grouping Act of that year, it became the responsibility of the London Midland & Scottish and Southern Railways. However, it was always known by its original name – possibly because it was invariably referred to as 'the Slow and Dirty' or the 'Slow and Doubtful', nicknames it never really managed to escape – and it continued to operate both a long-distance and local service up to the time of its closure in 1966. Many were the holidaymakers who travelled the line from the grimy industrial towns of the north to savour the sea air of the Dorset coast, en route passing through the lovely countryside of the Mendip Hills. Long-distance trains were usually well loaded, often requiring two locomotives to lift them over the heavily graded route through the Mendips. However, long stretches of single track could cause operating problems when, as frequently happened, a train suffered delay and lost its path in the timetable, leading inevitably to growing unpunctuality. The evocatively named *Pines Express*, which conveyed holidaymakers from Manchester to Bournemouth in the summer months, took most of the day to complete its journey, doubtless a pleasure for some but a test of endurance for others.

Sadly today there is little sign of this former route, no section of it having been preserved apart from three short stretches near Midsomer Norton. To the railway historian there is no sadder sight than an abandoned railway line with its dilapidated stations and overgrown embankments and cuttings, the latter often encroached by haphazard development or filled with refuse, all of which sully the memory of our Victorian ancestors who invested so much money and skill in building a transport system that was in its day a world-beater.

Wells Cathedral

A cathedral, the name of which derives from the five wells where the earliest settlement may have been founded nearly 2,000 years ago.

Look for the great scissor arches, the Jesse Window beyond the high altar, the west front, the chapter house and the spacious grounds of the Bishop's Palace.

There has been a religious community in Wells for more than a thousand years, early Christians having been drawn to the area by the springs of fresh water that gave the town its name. Once the smallest city in England and since the twelfth century dominated by its magnificent cathedral, Wells, often described as the 'capital of the Mendips', in earliest times relied for its wealth on mining and wool, as did many neighbouring towns of similar size in North Somerset.

Wells Cathedral could also be described as a world-beater. Built over a period of nearly 250 years in the English Gothic style it dominates all around it and symbolizes the faith and determination of our Christian forebears who, without any of the technical support that we enjoy in the twenty-first century, constructed a truly magnificent centre of worship. However, the first church in Wells was built in 705 at a site where, since time immemorial, five springs had provided water

The west front of Wells Cathedral.

to the people of the area. The land was given by Ina, a Saxon king of Wessex, to allow Aldhelm, the Bishop of Sherborne, to build that church. Two hundred years later, the church became a cathedral and the Diocese of Bath and Wells was created.

Wells was abandoned as the seat of the bishop when in 1089 his *cathedra* was moved to Bath Abbey on the orders of William the Conqueror. However, in 1174 work began on the present Wells Cathedral at a site to the north of the original Saxon church and in 1239 it was dedicated, with the Pope decreeing in 1245 that it should henceforth once again become the mother church of the Diocese of Bath and Wells. Early work had started in the quire and then progressed west into the nave. A break of ten years in the building of the nave can be identified by a change in the size of the blocks of stone; when work resumed technical improvements in how stone was handled meant that larger blocks were used and the transition from one size to another can be clearly seen halfway down the nave on both sides.

The west front of the cathedral is one of the finest of its kind. Limestone, quarried near Shepton Mallet, has weathered over the centuries with many of the carvings of religious and historical figures and biblical scenes losing definition, eroded by the prevailing west wind and rain; however, some have been recently re-carved. Amongst the many statues is that of Christ at the top of the west front with the twelve apostles below and Mary the Mother of Jesus at the bottom above the west door. Elsewhere on the façade are scenes from the Bible. The central figure in the row of apostles' statues is that of St Andrew, easily recognized by the large cross he is holding and selected for special identification since the cathedral is dedicated to him. There are nearly 400 statues at the western end of the cathedral, the largest such collection in Europe. The two towers flanking the central façade were added at a later date.

On my visit to the cathedral I was fortunate to be shown around by an old friend, now one of the Wells team of guides. He pointed out to me the holes made in the façade of the west front used to allow the choir and trumpeters to perform from within the cathedral in order to project their music to the outside. This happened on important Church feast days, in particular on Palm Sunday; as the clergy and worshippers processed across the Cathedral Green towards the cathedral, they would have been greeted by the voices of the choir and the sound of trumpets as they approached the west end. Imagine the surprise and pleasure with which such an outburst of music and singing must have been greeted by those in the procession.

Between the nave and the quire is the crossing, where the two transepts intersect with the main body of the cathedral, below the tower. The font, one of the last remaining relics of the original Saxon church, stands in the south transept and is still in use today a thousand years after its construction, although the carved figures of saints that once adorned it were removed when it was installed in the new Gothic cathedral. In the north transept is Wells Cathedral's original clock. Constructed 600 years ago to bring order to the liturgical routine of the cathedral, it has a twenty-four-hour face and images of knights that rotate every quarter hour. Like in so many cathedrals the Wells timepiece was the forerunner of a system that was to inject a greater measure of order into the lives of those who lived in medieval times.

The tower was built in the early years of the fourteenth century but when in 1313 Dean John Godelee decided to add an even higher level, problems quickly manifested themselves and the danger of collapse became imminent. The solution arrived at by the master mason of the day, William Joy, was to reinforce the tower with three scissor arches in order to spread the additional weight. His plan worked to perfection and the tower has remained stable ever since. Joy's scissor arches are unique in Christendom and they stand today as yet another demonstration of the imagination and resolve of our medieval ancestors. It is worth visiting Wells simply to view these remarkable examples of engineering.

Beyond the central tower the visitor enters the quire, dominated beyond the high altar by the Great East Window, or Golden Window. The window takes the form of a vine and depicts Christ's lineage growing out of Jesse, through his son King David, Solomon and Josiah to Mary the mother of Jesus, twenty-seven generations in all. The figures either side of the central lancet symbolize the kings of Judah and the prophets. There are many Jesse windows in England – York Minster has two – and indeed a greater number on the Continent, but that in Wells is possibly one of the finest. In a side aisle off the quire are the tombs of the seven Saxon bishops of Wells, whose remains were

The Bishop's Palace at Wells.

The scissor arches supporting the tower.

transferred there from the original church in the thirteenth century. Their presence reinforces the strong feeling of continuity that permeates every aspect of the history of Wells.

Beyond the high altar is the Lady chapel, completed in 1326. Much of the glass was vandalized by the Duke of Monmouth's troops, billeted in the cathedral before the Battle of Sedgemoor in 1685, and those pieces remaining were later put together in an arrangement that does not represent the original style of the windows. As the cathedral guide book explains, 'these windows remind us of the vandalism involved in much English church history and how much medieval beauty was destroyed, notably in the Civil War (1642–7) and Monmouth's Rebellion (1685).' To that observation should be added the damage visited on so many religious buildings during the Reformation, a hundred years before.

No description of Wells Cathedral would be complete without mention of either the chapter house or the Bishop's Palace. Sadly I was unable to visit the former because it was closed to allow filming to take place. From the account given in the official guide it is 'unique … one of the most glorious rooms in Europe … octagonal in shape with a central pillar that divides into thirty-two shafts, which soar into the ceiling like a fountain rising from the floor.' The staircase leading to the chapter house, worn away by the passage of feet since the end of the thirteenth century, is bordered by the oldest stained glass in the cathedral.

The palace moat.

The grounds surrounding the cathedral are amongst the most attractive in England. The moat, which must have once harnessed the waters from the original five springs, now surrounded by gardens, the grounds of the Bishop's Palace and the adjacent deer park all confirm that when built, Wells Cathedral was intended to be a religious foundation that would endure. And so it has as the seat of the Bishop of Bath and Wells, whose jurisdiction today broadly encompasses the county of Somerset, a splendid demonstration of how our ancestors with determination and rudimentary skills built a fine centre of worship and endowed it for the spiritual benefit of future generations.

The absence of a modern-day rail link to places as historically important as Wells is a matter of regret, especially in an age when travel by other means may one day become increasingly difficult. There have been several re-openings of railway routes nationally over the last thirty years but few of them have occurred in the counties of South West England. Nostalgia is not necessarily a good reason for trying to replicate the past, but those Victorians who constructed and operated the S&D and other railways to carry generations of travellers across the Mendips to celebrated places like Wells may have appreciated something that their Norman predecessors equally understood when building their great cathedrals. Both dynasties built their structures for a purpose and they built them to last. I sometimes wonder whether succeeding generations may occasionally have been too quick to dismantle the work of their gifted predecessors.

Wells Cathedral from the south.

Chapter 8

Gloucester and Bristol

Getting There

Both Gloucester and Bristol can be reached from Paddington Station in London. Journey times to both cities are about two hours. However, a fast train to Bristol Temple Meads Station can take little more than ninety minutes. Most journeys to Gloucester will require a change of trains at Swindon and time should be allowed for this. Trains between Gloucester and Bristol take less than an hour.

Railway Notes

You will by now be familiar with the name of Brunel who built the Great Western Railway during the middle years of the nineteenth century. One of his earliest projects was the construction of a route west from London following the valley of the river Thames almost as far as Swindon, a town the name of which has been synonymous with railways since the days of steam. At one time 12,000 people were employed there in locomotive building across 320 acres of workshops and sidings. It is at Swindon that the routes to Gloucester and Bristol diverge. Steam railways created Swindon as they did other railway towns in Britain like Crewe and Doncaster.

Since the late 1960s few publicly scheduled steam trains have run on Britain's railways although an increasing number of private, steam-hauled excursions are now permitted on certain lines. In addition there are now more than a hundred independently operated heritage lines, run by enthusiasts using tracks and stations once owned by British Railways. These keep alive the memory of how railways once operated and provide a unique insight into the early days of the Industrial Revolution. Amongst the best known lines are the Severn Valley Railway in the West Midlands, the West Somerset Railway, the Bluebell Railway in Sussex and the North Yorkshire Moors Railway. Most lines operate over the standard railway gauge.

The former Poet Laureate Sir John Betjeman loved steam trains and in the post-war years used his considerable powers of expression to try to influence those intent upon rationalizing the country's rail network in the interests of greater efficiency and faster speeds. In a tribute to Sir John in his book *John Betjeman on Trains*, Jonathon Glancey wrote, 'Betjeman loved trains not just for themselves, but because they were a wonderful way of travelling through Britain and looking out over ever-changing townscapes and countryside. He liked the often quixotic stories of Britain's railways, like that of the Great Central, which aimed, rather optimistically, for Paris via a Channel Tunnel a century ago. And then there was the Somerset and Dorset, hoping to win a slice of transatlantic traffic from the end of its meandering branch line to Burnham on Sea.'

Large numbers of people are today drawn to what might be described as the 'steam experience'. For them, as for Betjeman, steam trains never lose their appeal.

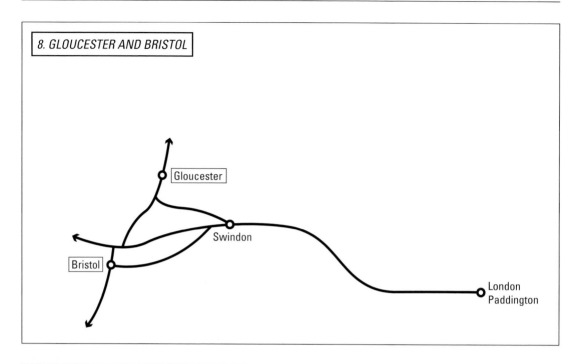

8. GLOUCESTER AND BRISTOL

Gloucester

Swindon

Bristol

London
Paddington

Statue of Sir John Betjeman at St Pancras International Station.

Gloucester Cathedral

It is the glory of a city where the cathedral was first founded as an abbey at the end of the eleventh century.

Look for the Crecy Window, the contrasting styles of the nave pillars, the tomb of Edward II, the Imjin River Memorial and the cloisters.

Gloucester was originally established by the Romans as a base from which they might invade Wales. *Glevum* was its Roman name and it stood on the banks of the river Severn. Today the city's greatest glory is its cathedral, built by the Normans and for 500 years the centre of a monastic settlement until 1541, when the abbey church was re-founded as a cathedral by Henry VIII. For me Gloucester Cathedral is not only the most beautiful of buildings but also a place of happy personal memories since I was married in its nave.

In 1072, Serlo, a monk from Normandy, was appointed Abbot of Gloucester by William the Conqueror and it was he who began the building of an abbey church there in the Romanesque style. The core of the building was completed between 1089 and 1260, with the nave finished first, followed later by the central tower in 1222 and a spacious Lady chapel in 1228, subsequently rebuilt around 1465. Meanwhile in the fourteenth century, the two transepts were remodelled and the quire, East Window and cloisters all finished.

You enter the cathedral by the south porch, which dates from the fifteenth century. Above the porch are statues of St Peter and St Paul with the four Evangelists; below and to the left at head height is a statue of Serlo. The first impression on arriving inside the cathedral is of the width and expanse of the nave with its vast Norman piers and relatively low roof. The two most westerly bays of the nave were rebuilt in

The south door of Gloucester Cathedral.

The nave.

The tower, Gloucester Cathedral.

King Edward II shrine.

the 1420s and replaced in the Perpendicular style by Abbot Morwent. The contrast between the two styles is very marked. About the same time, Morwent also demolished and rebuilt the west end of the cathedral.

Moving east through the screen and into the quire the layout is similar to other medieval cathedrals. The original rather dark Norman quire was converted into the present Perpendicular interior in the middle of the fourteenth century when Edward III ordered the building of a screen inside the original arcade, thereby considerably lightening the eastern part of the church. Approximately a hundred years later, the tower was also rebuilt.

Beyond the altar and its accompanying reredos is the Great East Window, a vast area of medieval stained glass built in the fourteenth century and intended to demonstrate the hierarchical nature of medieval society. At the top of the window stands St Gregory while below him is a cluster of angels. Beneath them in the centre of the window are Christ and the Virgin Mary flanked by the twelve apostles. The next tiers down depict saints and martyrs along with abbots and bishops, while in the very lowest tier are shown heraldic shields of royalty and noble families. The window is occasionally referred to as the Crecy Window since some of the families represented in the lowest tier would probably have fought for Edward III at the battle of Crecy in 1346 when, against all predictions, he defeated the French and went on to capture Calais. The window is Gloucester's crowning glory.

Royalty have been closely connected with Gloucester throughout history. Robert 'Curthouse', the eldest son of William the Conqueror, is thought to be buried somewhere under the cathedral. A man said to be both lazy and foolhardy, Robert, Duke of Normandy, was denied the English crown when his father died in 1087, his younger brother William seizing the throne instead. Four years later when William II died in a hunting accident, Robert again missed his opportunity to rule when his youngest brother, Henry, defeated him. Later Robert was captured by Henry I and confined to Cardiff Castle for the last twenty-eight years of his life. His effigy can be seen in the south ambulatory of the cathedral.

There is also the magnificent tomb of Edward II. Edward, who inherited a kingdom short of money and at war with the Scots, was tried for incompetence and deposed in 1327, thereafter being confined in nearby Berkeley Castle. He was murdered later that year, allegedly by being suffocated, possibly on the instructions of his wife. His magnificent tomb carved in alabaster is in the north ambulatory. Following Edward's

Cross carved by Colonel Carne while in captivity during the Korean War.

Effigy of Robert 'Curthouse', eldest son of William the Conqueror, in Gloucester Cathedral.

death a surge of emotion resulted in considerable riches being donated to the abbey church, allowing many of the changes to its east end and quire, already chronicled, to be undertaken.

These two stories and other anecdotes concerning the abbey church and the cathedral are recorded for the visitor through an imaginative scheme by which the visitor can view a tomb or memorial and then listen on a mobile telephone as the circumstances surrounding its history are recounted. There are seven stories in total, including one about Edward Jenner, a doctor and lifelong observer of birds and their migratory habits, who lived at Berkeley and discovered a vaccination against smallpox, a deadly disease until the twentieth century when it was formally declared to have been eradicated. Jenner died in 1823 and there is statue of him at the west end of the cathedral.

Another account concerns those members of the Gloucestershire Regiment captured by the Chinese at the Battle of the Imjin River in Korea in 1951. The ordeal of the regiment's chaplain is told in graphic detail and the stone Celtic cross, carved by the Commanding Officer, Colonel Carne, while in captivity, is on display in the north ambulatory opposite a memorial window unveiled in 1997.

Much of the glass in the cathedral is Victorian or later, some by Charles Kempe. The fourteenth-century Great East Window has already been described but you should also visit the south ambulatory chapel to view the vividly painted blue window by Tom Denny, which tells the New Testament story of Thomas in the presence of the risen Christ. The window was commissioned in 1989 as part of the 900th anniversary celebration of Serlo's building of the abbey church. The longer you look at the window the more you will see in it.

Gloucester's final gem is its cloisters, an area where the monks would have lived, worked and studied in medieval times. The places where their desks were positioned and the *lavatorium* where they washed can all be seen. Cloisters were usually built on the south or warmer side of an abbey but for some reason at Gloucester they were located to the north.

The cathedral dominates the city and rises above the surrounding buildings. Located not far from the banks of the river Severn, it can be seen from most directions before the city is reached; from the Cotswold escarpment to the south, from May Hill to the north and from the high ground that must be crossed when approaching from the Forest of Dean and Wales to the west. It is no wonder the Romans chose such a strategic position for a settlement 2,000 years ago and that the Normans later confirmed it as an ideal location for an important abbey.

The east or Crecy Window at Gloucester Cathedral.

Railway Notes

Forty miles south of Gloucester lies the port city of Bristol, reached in less than an hour by train. Bristol, a mercantile centre and the starting point for many expeditionary voyages to the Americas and other parts of the New World from the seventeenth century onwards, has been a major trading and manufacturing centre for generations. Communications played their part in such developments and here too Brunel used his engineering skills, not only to design and build railways but also to construct the docks, which he rebuilt in 1831, and later ocean-going ships. Strangely there is no memorial in the cathedral to the man who gave so much to the city.

Temple Meads Station could well be described as a railway cathedral. In 1841 the railway from London arrived in the city and Brunel constructed a large, cavernous train shed with a glass roof and a Gothic-style frontage traversing the many tracks running past the platforms. The structure remains largely unaltered although part of the station on the west side is today unused; even so, Brunel would no doubt still recognize his architectural masterpiece of nearly 200 years ago.

One of Britain's heritage railways. A North Yorkshire Moors Railway train at Goathland.

Temple Meads Station, Bristol. (NRM)

Bristol Cathedral

A cathedral that reflects the history and culture of this mercantile city.

Look for the south transept with its steps leading to the monks' night stairs and the nearby Saxon stone, the two Lady chapels, the memorial to Sidney Smith and the chapter house.

The cathedral stands in the centre of the city on College Green, an area of grass lawns surrounded by some imposing civic buildings. It was founded by Robert Fitzhardinge of Berkeley Castle in 1140 as the church of an Augustinian abbey. When later widowed, Fitzhardinge became a canon in the cathedral he had originally founded. Little of his abbey church remains other than, at the west end, the Norman gatehouse and the fine chapter house to the south. Although close to several imposing buildings and with traffic constantly circulating, the cathedral stands strangely undiminished by the sights and sounds of the city.

Having been built by the Normans, Bristol Cathedral might originally have looked similar to its counterpart at Gloucester. However, over a period from the thirteenth to the fifteenth centuries

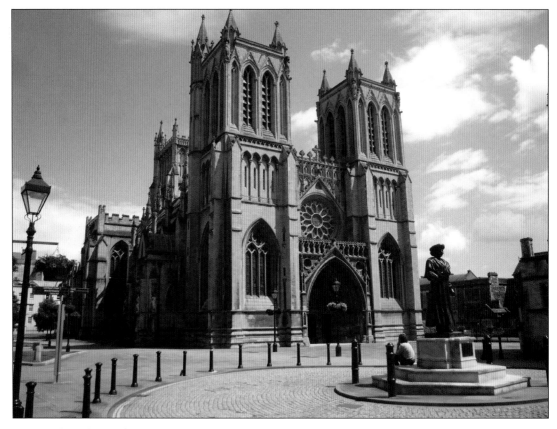

The west front, Bristol Cathedral.

The nave, looking east to the quire.

the original abbey church was extensively altered, being gradually restructured to become a building more representative of the Gothic style. The last of these changes was in progress at the beginning of the sixteenth century when plans were made to demolish the nave of the abbey church and replace it in a more modern style; before that work could begin Henry VIII launched his Reformation and in 1539 the abbey church was closed. Vigorous lobbying then ensued to allow Bristol to become the centre of a diocese, this being agreed in 1542 with the church being reinstated as the cathedral of the new Diocese of Bristol. The nave was not, however, rebuilt until towards the end of the nineteenth century.

When rebuilt the aisles of the nave were constructed at the same height as the rest of the building and as a result the whole cathedral appears as one unified structure with windows reaching almost to the roof. This provides much more light than in most cathedrals, the resulting building being known as a 'hall church'. This is said to have occurred because of the delay in rebuilding the nave; the Victorian architects were therefore able to adopt practices similar to those used originally by their medieval predecessors. The ribs of the vaulting in the roofs throughout the cathedral make intricate patterns and are known as lierne vaults. If you look up you will see these vaults and also the roof bosses, which differ from one part of the cathedral to another.

There are many memorials along the walls and on the floor of the cathedral. In the north transept there is a particularly striking tablet commemorating the life of Sydney Smith, a clergyman and

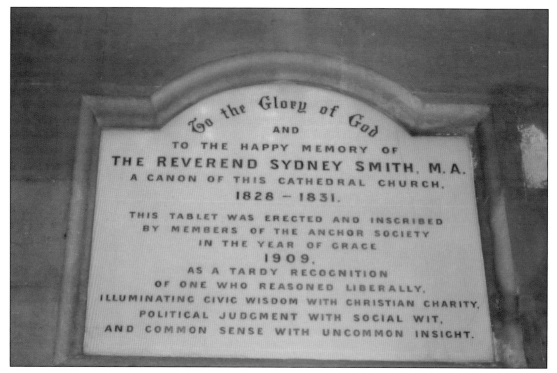

Memorial commemorating Sydney Smith.

man of letters and a Canon of Bristol from 1828 to 1831. Belatedly erected in 1909, the memorial expresses Smith's distinction in the following words: '… a tardy recognition of one who reasoned liberally, illuminating civic wisdom with Christian charity, political judgement with social wit, and common sense with uncommon insight.' Today Smith still remains an important figure to his adherents in the Sydney Smith Society.

Bristol has two Lady chapels. The Elder Lady Chapel, built in 1220, predates the main part of the present cathedral, being the first Gothic addition to the abbey church. It was originally separated from the main church and was designated 'elder' in 1298 when a second Lady chapel was built at the east end. The construction of this second chapel marked the beginning of the main programme to gradually rebuild the abbey church in the Gothic style.

As you walk around the east end of the cathedral you will come to the south quire aisle and the Berkeley Chapel built in memory of the family of that name who are also associated with Gloucester Cathedral. In the vestibule leading to the chapel there is an alcove where bread to be used for the communion service was originally baked. It is located opposite a recess that contains the Bishop's crozier, or pastoral staff.

A narrow stairway leads off one corner of the south transept, which reminds us of the days when the monks lived in dormitories above the cloisters, from where they would descend at all hours of the day or night to take part in services in the quire. The steps are well worn and must have been tramped by many thousands of feet. Close by the stairs is the Saxon Stone, one of Bristol's great treasures, said to be older than the cathedral and dating from pre-Norman times. It is now set into

The north side of Bristol Cathedral.

the transept wall. On it, Christ, wearing a halo, is shown as a triumphant figure contemplating the underworld of hell while trampling the Devil and a serpent. He is seen drawing towards him a figure, possibly Eve, the mother of the human race, thereby removing her from the clutches of Evil. He holds her tight to prevent her from slipping. Where the stone came from is unknown, it being found in 1831 when a fire led to its discovery under the floor of the chapter house.

It is claimed that the chapter house at Bristol is the finest example of such a building of the Norman era. Built in 1165, the room is decorated with several different designs and patterns, with niches along the walls built to accommodate seats. It is used today, as it always has been, for meetings of the cathedral authorities, the Dean and Chapter or previously the College of Canons. Earlier still the monks would have gathered there to read a chapter of the bible or other relevant religious works before getting down to business, hence its name. This great room was nearly lost in 1831 when a mob, vexed with the bishop for his opposition in the House of Lords to the passing of legislation designed to ensure electoral reform, burned his palace and tried to destroy the chapter house as well. Only the courageous actions of the Head Verger, William Phillips, prevented them from doing so. A memorial to him is in the south transept.

Midlands

Coventry Cathedral.

Hereford Cathedral.

Chapter 9

Hereford and Worcester

Getting There

There are three routes linking London to Hereford and Worcester. The first from Paddington uses a direct service, requires no change of trains and takes two-and-a-half hours to reach Worcester, with another forty-five minutes to Hereford, where the train terminates.

Both alternative routes require a change of trains. Paddington to Newport (South Wales) takes two hours, with a connecting service to Hereford a further three-quarters of an hour.

A third option is to travel on a Pendolino tilting train from Euston to Birmingham, a journey of ninety minutes, and then to change onto a local train to Worcester and Hereford. The journey time from Birmingham to Worcester is an hour.

Actual journey times for the latter two routes will depend upon the feasibility of the train connections.

Railway Notes

Chapter 16 discusses some of the proposals of the 1960s' Beeching report setting out a future structure for Britain's railways, which resulted in the country's network being reduced to a core of 11,000 miles. The unforeseen consequences of some of the closures recommended subsequently came to be recognized and many were reversed by successive governments. However, there still remain a number of routes that experience suggests should not have been removed from the railway map by Beeching and that, fifty years afterwards, might be reinstated to the advantage of local communities.

Thirty years later in the mid 1990s, the Government decided that it should remove itself from the direct provision of rail services; after a lengthy and complicated legislative process the running of trains was delegated to the private sector while control of track and the infrastructure was retained as a quasi-public service. At the time there was an expectation that an injection of private capital would result in much needed investment in the rail infrastructure and a consequent raising of operational standards. Some people even envisaged a loosening of financial control by the Treasury, encouraging a more entrepreneurial approach to the running and marketing of services. Over the fifteen years since privatization, improvements to the nation's railways have tended to concentrate on the principal routes carrying the majority of passengers and freight. More lightly used rural lines have generally received less investment, with track and infrastructure renewals only being carried out when deemed to be unsafe or life-expired. Overall privatization still has a long way to travel before the full fruits of the original political initiative will be felt.

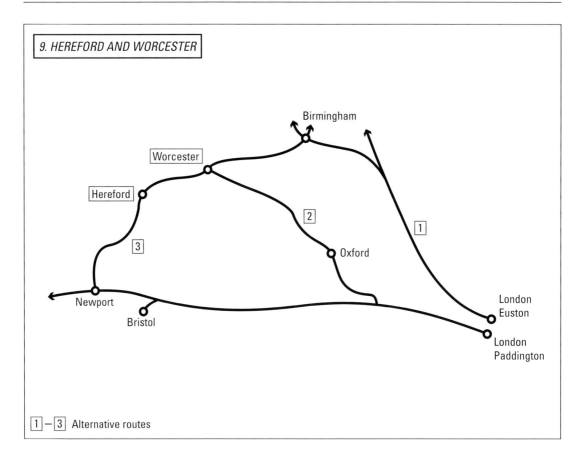

9. HEREFORD AND WORCESTER

Birmingham

Worcester

Hereford

2

1

3

Oxford

Newport

Bristol

London
Euston

London
Paddington

1 – 3   Alternative routes

A Worcester to London express in the Cotswolds.

The journey from London to Hereford and Worcester by whichever route illustrates this contrast in operational performance. The direct service from Paddington traverses the lovely North Cotswold countryside but is not fast by mainline standards, despite investment in infrastructure now taking place to shorten journey times. The two alternative routes, changing at either Birmingham or Newport, provide fast and comfortable journeys to those two places but the connecting services tend to be slow, uncomfortable and inconvenient, especially if a train change is missed.

Around Worcester and between there and Hereford I felt I was travelling in a railway time warp. Great Western-style stations, many unchanged since the days of steam, slow running and track rationalization seemingly undertaken more to reduce costs rather than to permit higher speeds, all gave the impression of a second-class system. I hope that in time there will be a change in attitude since reliable service provision is important to local people and could bring considerable benefits both economically and environmentally.

Hereford Cathedral

Hereford's fortifications were built in the eighth century to protect the Saxons from Welsh invaders.

Look for the misericords and the choir stalls in the quire, the *Hereford Gospels* and other historic books in the chained library and Hereford's *Mappa Mundi* on display in a room off the cloisters.

Hereford Cathedral across the river Wye.

Hereford Cathedral.

I visited Hereford on a damp and overcast November day. The city, well known as a centre for fruit-growing and the brewing of cider, is not an attractive place although its Norman cathedral, standing on the banks of the river Wye, bestows a sense of solid majesty.

Churches existed in Hereford in Saxon times. Ethelbert, an early bishop, built a stone church there before he was brutally murdered in 794 by King Offa of Mercia for reasons not entirely clear but may have had something to do with his wish to marry Offa's daughter. Miracles later came to be associated with Ethelbert's tomb and he was eventually canonized. Today's cathedral is jointly dedicated to St Ethelbert and to St Thomas Cantilupe. Ethelbert's statue stands to the right of the high altar while St Thomas's tomb is in the north transept.

The present cathedral dates from 1107 when building began to replace previous churches in the city. Predominantly Norman in style, areas of the original construction can be found in the south transept, the crossing, in parts of the west front of the nave and at the baptismal font. Later development led to the building of the quire, the ambulatory and the Lady chapel in the thirteenth century and the massive central tower a hundred or so years later. Further changes took place in Victorian times when considerable modification was necessary to save the cathedral from decline.

Bishop Thomas Cantilupe, a well-respected prelate of the thirteenth century, found himself in dispute with the Archbishop of Canterbury in 1280 over legal rights. Excommunicated by his archbishop, he journeyed to Rome to plead his case before the Pope but died on the way. His bones were brought back to Hereford and buried in a tomb where people later claimed miracles occurred. A shrine built in the Lady chapel in 1349 was destroyed at the time of the Reformation in 1540, following which a second tomb was placed in the north transept, where it remains to this day. Such was St Thomas's reputation that his original shrine became a focus for pilgrimage and it is believed that much of the money needed to build the central tower was bequeathed by pilgrims visiting and praying at Thomas's shrine.

When originally built the nave would have been a dark and rather forbidding place since little light was allowed to penetrate the interior. Two hundred and fifty years after its completion, windows were inserted into the clerestory layer of arches, allowing light to penetrate the gloomy sandstone interior and resulting in it becoming a more appealing place. In 1786 the west end of the nave collapsed and James Wyatt undertook repairs that led to the elimination of one bay. However, Wyatt's changes were not universally accepted and in 1908 a new front was built. Its window shows Christ in majesty accompanied by the Virgin Mary and St Ethelbert and was commissioned by the women of the diocese in 1908 to commemorate Queen Victoria's reign.

A screen had originally been built between the nave and the quire in order to emphasize the hallowed nature of the quire as the place where daily worship was conducted and the bishop had his seat. In the nineteenth century the screen was removed and the imposing Willis organ with its brightly decorated pipes, which was positioned on top, was moved to a new position high up on the south side of the quire. Below the organ and either side of the quire are the intricately carved

The nave of Hereford Cathedral.

choir stalls with their accompanying misericords, fashioned in the fourteenth century, some of the finest in the country.

East of the high altar is the Lady chapel, added in the early thirteenth century along with the crypt below. The chapel, light and welcoming, is in marked contrast to the rest of the cathedral, which tends to be of a more sombre disposition. There is much to study in the Lady chapel including Bishop Audley's chapel, which he built in order that prayers might be said for him after his death. However, his circumstances altered and after serving as Bishop of Hereford he moved to Salisbury, where it is said another chapel had to be provided for the same purpose.

Hereford possesses some wonderful treasures. The chained library, now housed in a specially built room off the cloisters, contains more than 1,500 books and manuscripts, including some of the oldest printed books dating from around 1473. The eighth-century Hereford gospels and one of four copies of the revised *Magna Carta*, written in 1217, are also displayed in the building. Chapter 5 describes Salisbury Cathedral's original *Magna Carta*, written in 1215 following the Treaty of Runnymede. The version of the same document in Hereford is a revised copy made after the death of King John and once Henry III had succeeded to the throne.

Hereford's finest possession must be the *Mappa Mundi*. Literally a 'cloth of the world', it is thought to have been designed towards the end of the thirteenth century by Richard of Haldingham and Lafford in Lincolnshire. The map seeks to show God's creation in a geographic context and is surprisingly accurate considering the limits of people's understanding of the extent of the world's surface and its physical features at that time. Jerusalem is in the centre of the map, which extends into Asia, North Africa and all of Europe. Easily recognized place names appear, although not always correctly correlated with one another. Drawings of kings, people and animals, both real and legendary, all appear in abundance, as do descriptions of annual events such as the harvest. The map provides a wonderful insight into to how the geography of the world was understood in the Middle Ages and is a must if you are visiting Hereford.

Worcester Cathedral

The cathedral stands high above the river Severn and is where King John is buried.

Look for the Norman crypt and try to find the whereabouts of those famous men commemorated in the cathedral.

The development of the Christian faith in Worcester took much the same form as in neighbouring Hereford. A diocese was first established in the late seventh century when Bosel was consecrated bishop and built a cathedral. Three hundred years later, Oswald founded a monastic settlement and constructed a church close to that of Bosel. In addition to the establishment of a monastery in Worcester, Oswald also founded a number of other monastic communities in Worcestershire before going on to become the Archbishop of York in 962, an appointment he held in parallel with his Worcester bishopric.

Following the Norman invasion of 1066, Bishop Wulfstan, appointed four years earlier, continued in office, the only Saxon bishop permitted to do so by William I. He had originally been prior of the monastery before becoming bishop and in 1084 starting work on the present

The south side of Worcester Cathedral.

The west front.

cathedral, which stands above the river Severn on its eastern bank. Unfortunately, not much of the work of Wulfstan's time is evident today.

Wulfstan's plans began at the east end with the building of the crypt, a spacious area beneath the quire and one of the largest remaining Norman crypts in England.

Thereafter work proceeded until the Norman cathedral was completed towards the end of the twelfth century. In 1216 King John died, a year after he had been compelled to agree the terms of the *Magna Carta* at Runnymede, and at his own request was buried in Wulfstan's cathedral, Worcester seemingly being a place he much loved. His tomb, upon which his effigy is flanked by miniature figures of St Wulfstan and St Oswald, stands just below the steps to the high altar in the centre of the quire. It could originally have been brightly painted and studded with jewels.

Close by King John's tomb on the south side of the quire is a chantry chapel built in 1504 by Henry VII and dedicated to his eldest son, Prince Arthur, who had died two years earlier shortly after marrying Catherine of Aragon. Catherine later became the first of the six wives of Henry VIII, Arthur's younger brother. Following her failure to provide Henry with a son and the Pope's subsequent rejection of Henry's petition to be allowed to divorce her, Catherine was excluded from the royal court. She died in 1536 and is buried in Peterborough Cathedral. Had Arthur not died so young he would have succeeded to the throne and the course of English history and that of the Church might have been very different.

The Elgar Window.

In 1224 Bishop William de Blois began rebuilding Wulfstan's Norman cathedral in the Early English style. Starting with the Lady chapel the work moved west, with the tower and transepts being completed during the latter part of the thirteenth century.

A mixture of styles can be clearly seen in the arches of the nave, where those nearest the west end are twelfth-century Norman while those to the east are taller and more pointed, conforming with the Decorated period. In 1540 the Benedictine monastery was dissolved on the instructions of Henry VIII and considerable change to the interior of the cathedral resulted. Screens in the nave, the monks' stalls, statues and stained glass were either removed or damaged, destructive acts that occurred in a large number of English churches and cathedrals during the same period.

Worcester Cathedral was largely restored in the nineteenth century when a major programme was undertaken by Abraham Perkins, a local architect, and George Gilbert Scott, whose role as a Gothic Revivalist

King John's tomb.

The quire at Worcester.

architect emerges several times in this book. New windows were installed at both the east and west ends of the cathedral and the organ screen was removed from between the nave and the quire and replaced with an ironwork screen; this allows an uninterrupted view the length of the cathedral, which greatly adds to the enjoyment of a visit. The interior of the cathedral inspires with its elegance while the outside view of the west end standing high above the river Severn presents one of the most striking aspects of any cathedral I have visited.

One of the joys of visiting any church is to discover who is commemorated within its walls. This often means a plethora of bishops and deans of medieval or later periods, or local people who have dedicated themselves to serving their church and community. At Worcester there is the added joy of being able to view memorials to four men who have served their country with great distinction in recent times. In the centre of the nave is positioned a plaque set into the floor that commemorates Stanley Baldwin, three times prime minster of Great Britain in the twentieth century, while not far away in the north-west corner of the nave is the Gerontius Window, which recognizes the achievements of the composer Sir Edward Elgar. His musical setting of *The Dream of Gerontius* in John Henry Newman's poem reflecting upon the passage of the human soul from death to life in God is recalled in the window.

Further east near the north porch is the Hastings Window, recording the exploits of Sir Charles Hastings, a local doctor who established the British Medical Association in the early years of the nineteenth century. Another local man to find a place in the cathedral is the Reverend Geoffrey Studdert Kennedy, a First World War chaplain who became known to thousands of servicemen as 'Woodbine Willie' for the manner in which he would minister to them in the trenches, in one hand holding his bible while giving away Woodbine cigarettes with the other. Along with the Reverend Theodore Bayly Hardy, to whom, as recorded in Chapter 14, there is a charming memorial in Carlisle Cathedral, Studdert Kennedy was one of the most respected and inspiring of the chaplains to serve in the Great War.

Gloucester, Worcester and Hereford cathedrals join together on a rotational basis to host the Three Choirs Festival, an annual celebration of choral and orchestral music originally featuring the choirs of the three cathedrals. Started in the early eighteenth century, the festival has been expanded to include many other musical and choral groups and is today held each year in July or August. It is one of the world's oldest classical choral music festivals.

A GWR locomotive of the type that would have worked around Worcester and Hereford in the days of steam.

Chapter 10

Lichfield and Coventry

■ Planning and controlling train movements ■ **Lichfield Cathedral** ■ the Royal Maundy
■ **Coventry Cathedral** ■ 14 November 1940 and the rebuilding of the cathedral ■

Getting There

Both Lichfield and Coventry are easily reached from Euston by direct trains; Lichfield in
two hours and Coventry in one hour, by travelling on either a Pendolino 'tilting train' or fast
intercity service.

Travelling by train between Lichfield and Coventry is less easy. Any journey will need to
be via Birmingham New Street, where a change will be necessary. A suburban train from
Lichfield will take forty minutes to reach New Street Station while a train from there to
Coventry will take thirty minutes.

An alternative worth consideration would be to take a taxi or a bus between the two
cathedrals, which are no more than 25 miles apart.

Railway Notes

I have always been impressed by the skills of the train control staff. Fifty years or more ago the
task of planning train schedules was undertaken by men with a particular mathematical flair
who might, quite literally, sit with wet towels around their heads calculating journey times
and passing points. Their aim was to determine the most suitable itinerary for a train to ensure its
safe passage without impeding other services. It was always said that Bill Marsden, a mathematics
master at Eton College, rewrote the Great Western Railway timetable at the beginning of the
Second World War in order to accommodate all the extra military traffic and that he did so using
only his algebraic skills.

Today, computers greatly aid the planning process. The task of regulating the operation of
Britain's train services is performed by Network Rail, the body responsible for the maintenance
of the track and the safe running of thousands of trains every day. Network Rail scrutinizes the
plans of the train companies, drafted to allow them to meet their franchise commitments, and
makes whatever adjustments may be necessary to ensure that conflicts are avoided. Once agreed
the timetable is immutable.

The movement of individual trains is managed by controllers at selected points across the
network working through signalling and station staffs. A train's progress can be monitored from
the beginning to the end of its journey and, should it be delayed en route, the extent of any
delay can be quickly calculated. Pinch points will occur at various places along a train's route,
principally at junctions where lines join or diverge. In the event of a delay to a train a decision
may have to be made as to whether a service should be held to avoid penalizing others or allowed
to proceed in the hope that it may regain time. Such decisions are not taken lightly since if a train

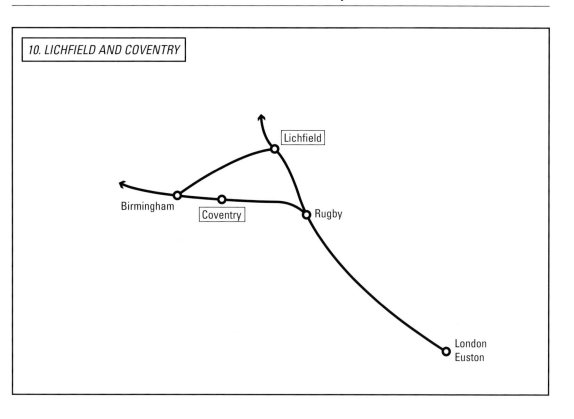

10. LICHFIELD AND COVENTRY

Lichfield

Birmingham

Coventry

Rugby

London
Euston

A Virgin Trains Pendolino on the West Coast main line. (NRM)

should lose its path in the timetable, the delays it suffers will accumulate and, in a worst case, affect not only itself but connections and return workings.

Delays to a service can arise for many reasons. It only needs a small incident – the failure of a carriage door to open properly, a disruptive passenger necessitating intervention by the railway police or the late arrival of a relief crew – and a train can quickly lose its allotted path. With so many more services using the railway network since privatization it should come as no surprise that saturation point is close to being reached on several mainlines and that plans to build a high-speed route to the north to create further capacity are being actively considered. Unlike the days when the whole network was used only by a single service provider, British Rail, there are today many companies operating trains, all of which may claim financial compensation from Network Rail should one of their services be delayed for reasons outside a company's control. Whether this is the best way to run Britain's railways is a question long debated but not yet satisfactorily answered.

Meanwhile, the physical control of a train travelling on a route is still undertaken using lineside indicators, either semaphore or colour light signals. Semaphores are slowly being replaced but they are still to be found on some more remote or less heavily used lines. In parts of Britain, notably the Highlands of Scotland and Mid Wales, radio signalling is also used, avoiding the need for signal structures. Automatic train control is widely deployed to ensure that, if a driver misreads a signal or fails to react to a warning, his train will be halted by an automatic application of the brakes. Chapter 4 explains how automatic train control works.

York Control Centre. (NRM)

Lichfield Cathedral

Only one of two English cathedrals with three graceful spires.

Look for the west front with its hundred statues, the two-storey chapter house, the library containing the *Chad Gospels* and the recently discovered Lichfield Angel.

L ichfield in Staffordshire has been a centre of Christian worship for more than 1,300 years. In the seventh century, St Chad, who had been taught by St Aidan at Lindisfarne, came to the area and a church was built on the site of the present cathedral. Chad served as Bishop of Mercia from 669 to 672 after moving his bishopric from Repton in nearby Derbyshire to Lichfield.

After Chad's death Bishop Hedda completed a Saxon cathedral on the site in 700 but this church was replaced in its turn by a Norman Cathedral, built between 1085 and 1140, and later by the present Gothic cathedral, started in 1195 and completed in 1340. This sequence of events pertaining to the establishment of Lichfield Cathedral is not dissimilar to the history of York Minster, where research has shown that the present Gothic minster is the third or fourth church to be built in the city, again after Saxon and Norman minsters. Much later, Lichfield suffered

The east end of Lichfield Cathedral.

The west front.

The Chad gospels.

considerable damage at the time of the Reformation, when St Chad's Shrine was destroyed, and during the period of the Civil War in the seventeenth century. Major restoration took place in the second half of the nineteenth century.

Lichfield Cathedral is in many ways unlike any other English cathedral. Built of sandstone and now in places almost black in appearance, it dominates Lichfield, which must be one of the smallest cathedral cities in Britain. The cathedral's three soaring spires, two above the west front and the third above the central tower, were built in the Early English style and their configuration is unique. They give the appearance more of a Continental cathedral than an English one. The full impact of the building can be best assimilated by observing it by standing well back from outside the west door, above which are arcades containing statues of the saints and the early kings of England.

The cathedral is distinctive in a number of ways. The chapter house, completed in 1249, is a two-storey octagonal structure, the only one of its kind. Originally used for gatherings of the bishop and his clergy it is today still used for meetings, receptions and concerts. The library on the upper floor houses the *Chad Gospels*, which are dated to 730. Written on vellum the 236 pages record the gospels of St Matthew and St Mark and part of the book of St Luke. This has led to speculation that there may have been a second volume containing the other half of St Luke's

The west window.

gospel and that of St John. Also in the chapter house is a glass case containing the remains of the Lichfield Angel, a sculpture dated from about 800 that it is believed may be a likeness of St Chad. It was discovered when a mechanical platform beneath the nave altar was constructed in 2003 and the area around it excavated.

The *pedilavium*, or vestibule, leading to the chapter house from the north quire aisle is thought to have been an area where in medieval times the biblical custom of 'masters washing their servants' feet' took place. The custom continues today on Maundy Thursday in Holy Week.

Maundy Thursday is an important day in the life of the Anglican Church since it is on that day that the Royal Maundy is distributed by the Sovereign. Each year a service is held in one of the forty-three dioceses in England, either in a cathedral or another important church, or in a church in the other parts of the United Kingdom, when a number of men and women, both groups totalling the years of age of the monarch, are presented with the Royal Maundy, a collection of coins contained in a small bag. The ceremony goes back to the reign of King John in 1210 and records show a continuous distribution since the time of Edward I. Originally the Maundy service included the washing of feet while the ceremony derives its name from the Latin word *mandatum*, meaning 'commandment', reflecting the service's opening words, which are contained in the Gospel of St John, Chapter 13: 'Jesus said: I give you a new commandment: Love one another; as I have loved you, so you are to love one another.' Recipients of the Maundy coins, which are legal tender, tend to be pensioners selected for their commitment to the Church and the community. Nobody who has received any other award is eligible.

The Royal Maundy was last distributed in Lichfield in 1988; in 2012, the year of Elizabeth II's Diamond Jubilee, York Minster was the chosen venue. Along with many other people from across the diocese and the Church more generally, I had the privilege of being present on that occasion, at what was the most wonderful and uplifting of services.

Reverting to Lichfield Cathedral there are numerous monuments to those serving in local regiments including an unusual one to Hodson's Horse, an Indian Army cavalry regiment that served in the ranks of the British Army from 1857 to 1947. Nearby in the south transept are a number of regimental colours laid up for safekeeping. Just a few yards from the transept is the Consistory Court where in former times the bishop would have sat in ecclesiastical judgement to hear offences committed by the clergy. Today the room is where the cathedral clergy gather to robe prior to a service. Standing inside the west end of the nave a visitor gets a magnificent view the length of the cathedral, made possible because all the roofs are the same height, culminating in the former Chapel of St Chad, now the Lady chapel.

At the time of my visit the East Window of Lichfield was stored to allow repairs to the stonework surrounding it. The Herkenrode Glass had been removed pending the renovation of the sandstone, which has suffered from pollution and condensation. The glass, made nearly 500 years ago by Flemish craftsmen, was transported to Lichfield in 1802 when Emperor Napoleon closed Herkenrode Abbey in Belgium. Its reinstatement is the subject of a major appeal.

There can hardly be a cathedral or major church in Britain today that does not find it necessary to appeal for the resources to secure its continuing survival. Stained glass, in particular the lead that assists in holding it in place, and surrounding stonework need regular checks to identify and rectify potential damage before it can escalate. No English cathedral benefits from direct government subsidy and it is left to the generosity of the public and, when deemed appropriate, the Heritage Lottery Fund to assist with the never-ending task of maintaining these hallowed buildings.

Coventry Cathedral

A city where the cathedral was destroyed by enemy action in 1940 and rose again twenty-two years later in a new building.

Look for the way in which the new building has been constructed to connect with the ruins of the old and walk through each to experience the spirit of reconciliation so powerfully represented in their juxtaposition.

The history of Coventry Cathedral is very different to that of Lichfield and I found my visit there on a bleak January day profoundly moving. The story of the destruction of the cathedral in 1940 and the immediate commitment by the Provost and Chapter to the building of a suitable replacement are part of the city and the nation's history. It is a story that cannot be told too often or that better illustrates the faith we mortals must place in our God.

However, it is first necessary to go back in time. In 1043 a Benedictine community was founded in Coventry by Leofric, the Earl of Mercia and his wife, Lady Godiva, who allegedly rode the

Coventry: the old and new cathedrals.

Graham Sutherland's tapestry *Christ in Glory*.

streets of the city naked to shame her husband into imposing less harsh taxes on the people. Godiva's statue stands prominently in Coventry today. Meanwhile, the Benedictine community had built its own church of St Mary and it is thought to have been Coventry's earliest cathedral. Standing close by St Mary's in the centre of the city were two other churches, Holy Trinity and St Michael's, the latter having probably been built in the twelfth century.

In the Middle Ages Coventry was a prosperous city and this was reflected in the size and grandeur of its churches. However, the Reformation initiated by Henry VIII caused St Mary's Church to fall into decline when the Benedictine priory was disbanded in 1539.

Previously in 1373 work had begun to enlarge St Michael's Church, built in the Perpendicular style with a magnificent spire, the third highest in England after those of Salisbury and Norwich cathedrals. Completed in 1460, the church fulfilled the role of a parish church until 1918, when the present-day diocese of Coventry was formed and St Michael's became its cathedral and the seat of its bishop.

Twenty-two years later on 14 November 1940, during the Second World War, the German Luftwaffe mounted Operation Moonlight Sonata, a major bombing raid on the Midlands, with Coventry the principal target. The city was saturated with incendiary bombs and much of the centre soon became an inferno, resulting in the loss of nearly 600 lives and the destruction of many buildings. St Michael's Cathedral was completely gutted but miraculously the tower, the

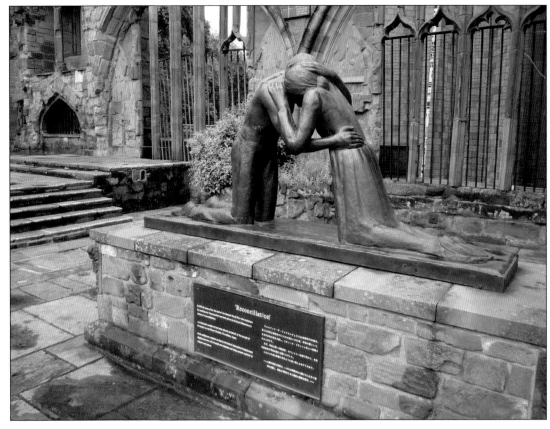

Josefina da Vasconellos' statue *Reconciliation*, in the ruins of the former cathedral.

spire and the outside walls remained in place. The attack was one of the most controversial events of the Second World War and one of the first occasions when a civilian population was deliberately targeted. Saturation bombing may at the time have had perceived military aims but the targeting of civilian populations can never be morally justified. Coventry in 1940 became a symbol of the intense pain felt by Britain; later the bombing of the German city of Dresden in 1945 by the Allied air forces provoked equally strong sentiments of revulsion and condemnation.

In the aftermath of the attack of 14 November those responsible immediately rallied to the task of restoring their cathedral. The Provost, the Reverend Dick Howard,

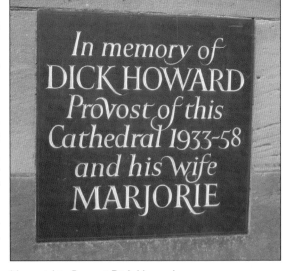

Memorial to Provost Dick Howard.

Epstein's *St Michael and the Devil*.

John Piper's baptistry window with the font below.

gently steered people's reactions away from bitterness and anger against the enemy and took positive steps to promote the notion of the need for forgiveness. As they walked through the ruins he and Jock Forbes, the cathedral's stonemason, reinforced this message by their respective acts; Forbes by taking two charred pieces of timber, binding them together in the shape of a cross and placing them in the ruined sanctuary of the cathedral while Provost Howard inscribed the simple words 'Father, forgive' on the blackened wall behind.

Within a period of a day and led by Provost Howard, it was proposed that a new cathedral would be built next to the ruins of St Michael's. Work did not begin until 1956 when HM The Queen laid the foundation stone of the new building, which was to be constructed at right angles adjacent to the ruins of the old cathedral. The new cathedral faces north although, for reasons of liturgy, the north end is referred to as the east end while the west end, which adjoins the ruins of St Michael's geographically, faces south. A competition was held to select the most appropriate design for the new cathedral and more than 200 architects submitted their ideas. Eventually the design proposed by Sir Basil Spence was selected, his theme being to portray the ruins of the old cathedral as a Sacrifice while the new building would rise like a phoenix from the ashes as a symbol of Resurrection.

The new cathedral of St Michael's was consecrated on 25 May 1962 amid celebrations of great joy and a desire that reconciliation should as far as humanly possible be consummated. It stands today as a memorial to those who have worked since the end of the war to put aside feelings of rancour and to embrace their former opponents in forgiveness and reconciliation. Benjamin Britten's *War Requiem* was performed for the first time a few days later.

A visitor to Coventry should walk from the railway station through the rebuilt city and past the more recently founded university to enter the cathedral at the Visitor Centre. Here there is an informative exhibition and a film explaining the horrors of 14 November 1940 and the ordeal that befell the Christian community that night. The visitor then enters the new cathedral through the Lady chapel, above which on the east wall of the cathedral hangs Graham Sutherland's huge tapestry *Christ in Glory*. The tapestry takes the place of an east window, weighs more than a ton and when first hung was the largest work of its kind in the world.

The cathedral interior is laid out on traditional lines using a design more or less similar to that followed by the great church builders of the past. There are, however, no transepts. As I walked past the high altar and down the quire towards the nave I was struck by the stark simplicity of the building, its clean lines, uncluttered space and soaring arches. The Baptistry Window designed by John Piper displays in vivid colours the 'Glory of God flooding into the World'; in front of it is placed the baptismal font, a rough boulder brought from a hillside near Bethlehem. The west end glass screen, through which can be seen the north side of the ruined cathedral only a few yards away, was engraved by John Hutton, a New Zealander, and shows angels, saints and Christian figures from the past.

Reflecting on my visit I believe that I should have perhaps first walked through the ruins of the old cathedral and then entered the new cathedral through the main entrance where, on one wall, there is placed Sir Jacob Epstein's sculpture, *St Michael and the Devil*. I would then have progressed up the aisle to stand in front of the high altar and below the Sutherland tapestry. That would have been the logical way to proceed since I would have travelled from the past to the present, my visit culminating in the Lady chapel dominated by the *Christ in Glory* tapestry. However, because the visitor entrance led me to enter the cathedral from the north or east end and walk towards the nave, I left the new building past the west screen and walked the few yards to the ruins of the old cathedral. I was glad that I had gone that way because, after moving through the new building, I found standing in the ruins of the old very poignant. To survey the weather-beaten walls and contemplate all that had happened there seventy years before, remembering how people had come to terms with what had occurred and how they had risen above their distress to build a new beginning, seemed to put everything in perspective.

The ruins have been left virtually as they were after November 1940 with a simple wooden cross in the devastated chancel and Josefina de Vasconcellos's sculpture showing a man and woman embracing in reconciliation. The statue was given to the cathedral in 1995 to mark the fiftieth anniversary of the end of the Second World War; at the same time a similar statue was placed in the Peace Park at Hiroshima in Japan, given by the people of Coventry.

I found it difficult to summarize my feelings after visiting Coventry Cathedral and will leave it to the words of the Provost in his welcome in the cathedral guide book. He has written the following, which I am sure will strike a chord in the minds of every visitor who goes to Coventry:

To move from the bombed ruins into the new cathedral building is to walk from Good Friday to Easter, from death to new life, from the jagged reminder of man's inhumanity to the soaring architecture that lifts the heart. I hope that, along with me, you want to say 'Thank God'.

The ruined cathedral seen through John Hutton's engraved glass screen.

North West

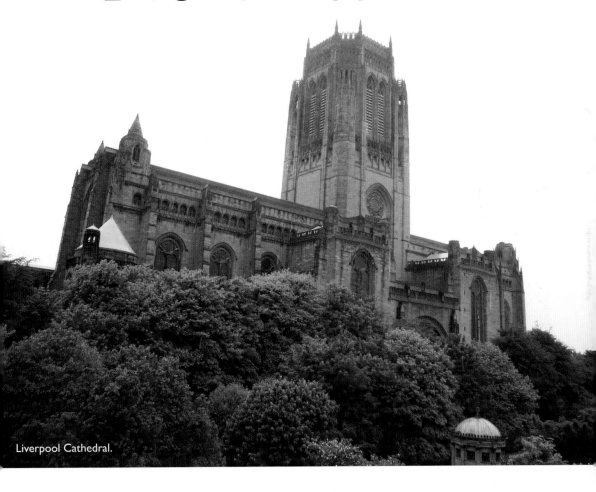

Liverpool Cathedral.

The central tower and cloisters, Chester Cathedral.

Chapter 11

Manchester and Chester

■ Crossing the Pennines ■ **Manchester Cathedral** ■ a railway run by a committee
■ **Chester Cathedral** ■

Getting There

A fast train from Euston to Manchester's Piccadilly Station will take about two hours. Chester can also be reached by a similar West Coast service from Euston, some trains proceeding direct to the city while others may require a change at Crewe.

There are two principal stations in Manchester and the traveller between there and Chester has a choice of two routes. Trains from Piccadilly take seventy-five minutes while those from Victoria Station, about an hour. Trains on both routes are provided with basic rolling stock and are neither very comfortable nor very fast.

Manchester can be easily reached from other parts of the country and the city is currently being developed as a major transport hub with expanded rail and bus services.

Railway Notes

Rather than concentrating on the railway approaches to Manchester from London and the south, this chapter describes how trains reach the city from Yorkshire and the towns to the east of the Pennines, a route of altogether greater interest and considerable potential as a major transport link.

The railway from North East England to Manchester passes through some of the major towns and cities of West Yorkshire before crossing the Pennine Hills at Standege. It provides one of three main Trans Pennine rail routes. Originally owned by the Lancashire and Yorkshire Railway Company it opened in the middle of the nineteenth century. If future plans materialize it could become the principal route for carrying passengers, freight and minerals across the Pennines, connecting the towns and ports of North East England and Yorkshire with the heavily industrialized conurbations of Lancashire and the port of Liverpool. As a railway artery it is as important as many of the routes radiating to all corners of the country from London. It may eventually be incorporated into the planned network of high-speed routes designed to modernize Britain's inadequate transport infrastructure.

The line runs parallel to the Huddersfield Narrow Canal for much of the latter's 20-mile course. Originally built in the eighteenth century to handle textile traffic, the canal was abandoned at the end of the Second World War but was revived in 2001, principally to cater for leisure craft. The canal and the railway come together to cross the Pennines at Standege Summit, where parallel tunnels, each 3 miles long, accommodate both transport systems. There were originally four tunnel bores but two were later abandoned. It must be hoped that if the railway is upgraded, one of the redundant tunnels might be reopened to permit the line to be again quadrupled to create greater capacity. Meanwhile, the canal tunnel carries pleasure traffic under conditions of strict

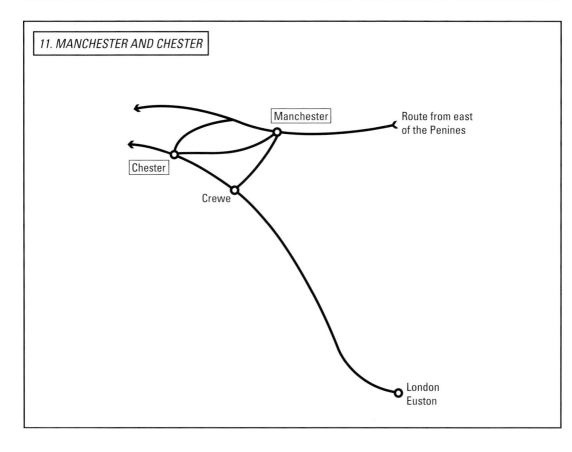

11. MANCHESTER AND CHESTER

Manchester

Route from east
of the Penines

Chester

Crewe

London
Euston

A locomotive that might regularly have been used on the Cheshire Lines routes.

control, a passage taking anything up to three hours. Before the advent of motor barges, boat traffic had to be propelled through the tunnel by 'leggers' using their legs to push against the tunnel roof thereby thrusting their barges forward. Once at the other end of the tunnel, barges were again hitched up to their towing horses, which would have been walked across the hills above the tunnel.

The wild moorland and steep valleys either side of the line house a number of mills built in the eighteenth century to process wool or, on the Lancashire side, cotton. Water power utilizing the abundant fast-flowing rivers and streams to drive looms was an essential element of the Industrial Revolution and changed the face of the countryside, dramatically transforming the lives of those who lived there. Dark, forbidding mills, reminiscent of military barracks, many now redundant from their original use, are dominated by bleak hillsides grazed only by sheep, places often shrouded in mist where the wind never blows lightly. Crossing the Pennines by train makes one realize what our Victorian ancestors achieved when they discovered the technology and processes that led to the industrialization of Britain during the early years of the nineteenth century.

The approaches to Manchester take the traveller through a long swathe of industrial and suburban towns. Communities at Stalybridge and Guide Bridge once owed their existence to the textile trade of the seventeenth and eighteenth centuries. As dormitories for the great commercial city of Manchester to their west, they today fulfil a very different purpose.

Advertisement for the CLC. (NRM)

Manchester Cathedral

Originally a parish church, the cathedral today serves a large urban diocese.

Look for the bishop's *cathedra* with its carvings of kangaroos, the Fire Window in the chapel of the local regiment and the buildings of Chetham's School.

Manchester Cathedral is a long walk from the Piccadilly terminus although only a few yards from Victoria Station. The city's modern Metro system and abundant buses make moving around easy. The cathedral only became a cathedral in 1848, when the diocese of Manchester was formed, but the building's history goes back several centuries before that. Situated in what might be termed Manchester's medieval quarter, the cathedral is closely associated with nearby Chetham's Library, the oldest surviving public library in Britain. Founded in 1653 by Humphrey Chetham, a far-sighted Manchester merchant, his endowment included a hospital and a school for poor boys. Today the building is used by Chetham's School of Music.

The building housing the library was built in 1421, when it was used as a college for priests who were to serve nearby St Mary's Church, now the cathedral. In 1422 Henry V gave permission for the church to become a collegiate foundation although the endowment was revoked by Edward VI in 1549. A new charter was later obtained from Elizabeth I in 1578.

Much of the cathedral dates from the early fifteenth century although it is believed, from relics found when the south door was dismantled in 1871, that parts of the building may have originated in Saxon times. The Lady chapel is thought to date back to 1299. However, extensive changes took place in the fifteenth century and again in the nineteenth century, while in 1940 the cathedral sustained considerable bomb damage following a German air raid.

The quire stalls and misericords, dating from the fifteenth century, and other work undertaken by John Huntington, the first warden of St Mary's whose statue is at the west end, are of particular note. The bishop's *cathedra* includes carvings of kangaroos in memory of Bishop Moorhouse, an Australian and bishop of the diocese a hundred years ago. The Chapel of the Duke of Lancaster's Regiment was originally a chantry chapel, a place where in medieval times hymns were continuously sung, usually for

The west front of Manchester Cathedral.

A Saturday morning service in the nave of Manchester Cathedral.

The quire.

the souls of the departed. The regiment, following various amalgamations in the last century, is today the custodian of the traditions and records of several predecessor regiments, most of which originated in south and central Lancashire or Cumbria. The chapel was a target of an IRA bomb attack in 1996, which badly damaged the striking Fire Window built fifty years earlier. That damage has now been repaired.

In a city of modern buildings and brightly lit and busy shops, where the pace of life never seems to slacken, I found the area surrounding the cathedral to be an oasis of relative calm, if not tranquillity. When I visited on a Saturday morning having travelled to nearby Victoria Station, there was an inter denominational service in progress; judging by the enthusiasm of those involved it was obvious that the cathedral was being well used and had extended its friendship towards the people of the city who most needed its support and comforting presence.

The Fire Window.

Railway Notes

In the years before the 1923 grouping of railway lines into the 'big four' companies, a number of independent railways covered the country, competing with one another and often adopting dubious tactics when attempting to damage one another's business. As already examined in Chapter 3, the haphazard nature of railway development was partly responsible for allowing such situations to arise. Nevertheless, even before 1923 many amalgamations had taken place and in that year the Government decided that there should only be four main railway operating companies. It was a sensible and logical step.

An exception to the amalgamations of 1923 was the continued independence of a company named the Cheshire Lines Committee, which retained its own management structure until 1947 when Britain's railways were nationalized. The railway, which broadly provided links to other companies in Manchester and South Lancashire and on routes from Manchester to Liverpool and Chester, was always referred to as a committee and seldom as a railway. The fact that the CLC was linked to so many different companies and crossed several boundaries meant that it was probably easier not to absorb it into a bigger group. In any event it continued to run efficiently up until 1947, employing locomotives and rolling stock of mixed provenance from other companies.

The former CLC line to Chester leaves Piccadilly Station through the southern suburbs of Manchester, thereafter serving a succession of affluent commuter towns before crossing the Cheshire Plain to Chester. Having lived not far from that city as a child, I have fond memories of travelling there to school on trains hauled by a variety of steam locomotives that had originated in the workshops of both the London & North Eastern (LNER) and London Midland and Scottish (LMS) railway companies. LNER 'Director' class engines were the mainstay of the line for a number of years, while the LMS usually provided the rolling stock. In addition to carrying regular passenger traffic the line also generated several freight flows, many serving the chemical industries around Runcorn and Northwich.

Chester Cathedral

Contained within one of the best-preserved walled cities in England, the cathedral stands only a few miles from the border with Wales.

Look for the four mosaics on the north side of the nave, the magnificently carved fourteenth-century stalls in the quire, St Werburgh's shrine and the Greene memorial, and enjoy the cloisters garden.

Like York, the walled city of Chester was founded by the Romans in the first century AD. A legion, a force of about 10,000 soldiers, was based in the city, which was called *Deva*. In the seventh century the Saxons founded a church in Chester and around 200 years later the relics of St Werburgh were brought to the city. Werburgh, the daughter of a Mercian king whose territory included Chester, lived her life as a nun and is said to have carried out many acts to alleviate pain and suffering amongst her followers. After she died miracles were attributed to her and she was proclaimed a saint by popular approval. The City of Chester is dedicated to her and her shrine is at the west end of the Lady chapel of the cathedral. She is also shown in the Great West Window.

Chester Cathedral.

The nave looking towards the west window.

After the Norman Conquest William the Conqueror appointed his nephew, Hugh d'Avranches, to be Earl of Chester and to rule the county. Nicknamed 'Lupus' because of his wolf-like disposition, he quickly established the city as a major military and administrative centre and then turned his attention to organizing the conversion of the Saxon church into a Benedictine monastery. The oldest remnants of this building, begun in 1092, can be seen in an arch of the north transept. Building of the church continued until completion in about 1220, with the chapter house finished by 1250. Over the next hundred or so years several parts of the Romanesque church were rebuilt in the Gothic style or, as in the case of the south transept, enlarged, thereby making it disproportionate in size to the Norman north transept. The nave, the last part of the church to be built, was completed by the end of the fifteenth century.

In 1540, at the time of the Reformation, the monastery was dissolved by Henry VIII, who a year later decreed that its church should become Chester Cathedral. As a result the existing diocese of Lichfield, which stretched from the Midlands north as far as the Scottish border, was reduced in size. Much of the cathedral's medieval glass was destroyed in the middle of the seventeenth century because it was deemed to be inappropriate by the bigoted supporters of Oliver Cromwell. A good example of their pernicious actions can be seen in a memorial to Thomas Greene and his two wives in the south transept. They are shown with their hands cut off; such an act of mindless vandalism was apparently carried out because the figures had their hands clasped together

The chapter house window.

in prayer, a gesture associated with the Church of Rome and therefore anathema to Puritan zealots.

Since then much work has been undertaken to enhance the sandstone building, which is today the seat of the Bishop of Chester. Major restoration work began in 1830 and, as with so many medieval buildings, has continued in one form or another ever since, with, as elsewhere, Sir George Gilbert Scott being closely involved. At the same time some windows were again filled with stained glass. Around 1885, four mosaics were installed on the north side of the nave; these show Abraham, Moses, David and Elijah. The Great West Window, depicting some of the medieval saints, was built in 1961, replacing a Victorian window destroyed by a bomb twenty years before during the Second World War, the only damage suffered by the cathedral during that conflict.

The visitor entrance does not do justice to the cathedral, which has to be reached through a congested area adjacent to the shop, after which a visitor must walk along part of the cloisters before entering the nave through a side door. However, once inside the cathedral the atmosphere is light and airy despite the natural darkness of the sandstone. The south transept contains a number of mainly military memorials, including one to Jack Cornwell, the youngest serviceman to be awarded the Victoria Cross in the First World War. He sailed in HMS *Chester*, a light cruiser, and was killed at the Battle of Jutland. As might be expected there are many memorials to those who have over the years served in the ranks of the Cheshire Regiment.

The cloisters on the north side of the cathedral were the area where the Benedictine monks lived and studied, the stone desks at which they worked still being in place. The garden in the centre is a tranquil place and by the entrance to it is a small plaque, set in glass, which commemorates two

The west front and St Werburgh Street.

The east end and chapter house.

Cheshire men, George Leigh Mallory and Andrew Irvine, who never returned from their attempt to climb Mount Everest in 1924. Meanwhile a detached bell tower, completed in 1975, is located within the cathedral precincts. The bells were first rung the same year.

Chester Cathedral and the city in which it stands, both of which can trace their origins back to the Romans, have always been special places for me. The city with its famous 'rows' of shops arranged in two storeys with those on top echeloned above and behind those at street level, and its striking position on a bluff above the river Dee, was close to where I grew up. When my father died a service was held in the cathedral to commemorate his life, while my elder sister had previously been married there.

Chester Cathedral's twentieth-century bell tower. The bells were rung for the first time in 1975. (Stephen Craven, under the Creative Commons Licence)

Chapter 12

Liverpool

■ The growth and decline of two great ports ■ the Liverpool Overhead Railway ■ **Liverpool Cathedral** ■

Getting There

Pendolino express trains link Euston Station in London with Lime Street Station in Liverpool in a little over two hours.

Trains from either Manchester Piccadilly or Victoria Station to Liverpool take about an hour. The express service from Piccadilly offers the fastest journeys and the more comfortable trains, some taking less than an hour.

Liverpool can also be reached from Chester in forty-five minutes by travelling up the Wirral Peninsula on one of the modern third rail electric trains that connect the two cities through a tunnel under the river Mersey.

Railway Notes

The previous chapter followed the Trans Pennine route to Manchester from the east. The logical extension of that route is the onward journey to Liverpool, an ancient seafaring city first granted a charter by King John in 1207. Liverpool can be reached direct from London or as easily via Manchester. As explained above, there are two main routes linking Manchester and Liverpool. The older and slower line from Victoria Station takes the route of the original Liverpool and Manchester Railway opened in 1830. The line's opening ceremony, attended by the prime minister of the day, the Duke of Wellington, was marred by tragedy when William Huskisson, the local MP, seeking a conversation with the duke, approached the latter's carriage, inadvertently standing in the path of an approaching train. Fatally injured, he became the first casualty of a railway accident. As described in Chapter 3 there is a memorial to Huskisson in Chichester Cathedral, while another stands at Rainhill Station, where the accident occurred.

The alternative route from Piccadilly Station follows a more southerly alignment via Warrington and approaches Liverpool through the city's southern suburbs. It is the faster of the two routes, with fewer stops. Shortly after leaving Manchester it crosses the Manchester Ship Canal, a waterway completed in 1894 thereby enabling vessels of considerable tonnage to sail the 36 miles from the mouth of the river Mersey at Liverpool into the industrial heart of Manchester. The railway negotiates a high embankment at Irlam, where the canal, easily visible, is crossed.

Both Liverpool and Manchester were great ports in their day and for that reason attracted considerable railway investment. Liverpool's early maritime business was based upon the American cotton and tobacco trades and later West Indies' sugar.

At the same time, Liverpool, today doubtless to its shame, was for many years the principal port for vessels plying the Atlantic to carry slaves from West Africa to the Americas, a trade that

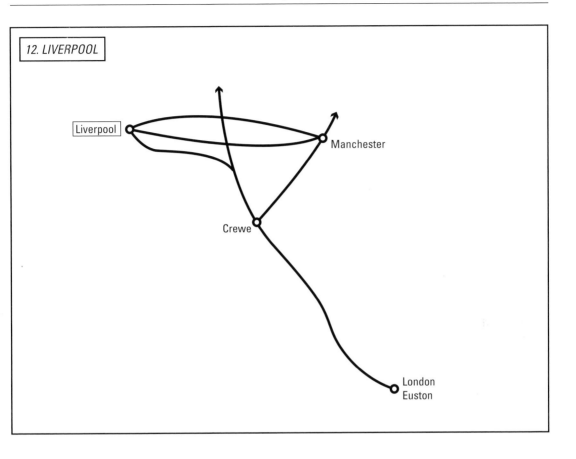

12. LIVERPOOL

Liverpool

Manchester

Crewe

London
Euston

did not finally cease until the early nineteenth century. More recently, the transatlantic routes with North America provided regular passenger traffic, including the carriage of thousands of emigrants intent upon starting a new life in the Americas in the middle of the nineteenth century. In its heyday the port was home to many shipping lines that sailed the world's oceans. Cunard, Blue Funnel Line, Elder Dempster and Bibby Line, all renowned names forty years ago, had ships based upon the port and they helped to sustain Liverpool's reputation as a major maritime centre right up to the 1960s. Thereafter growing competition from airlines and the introduction of containerization and new ship-handling technology, both developments the port's dockers were reluctant to accept, led to the gradual decline of the city's docks. More up-to-date ports such as Southampton and Felixstowe were the principal beneficiaries since they were prepared to accept more innovative working practices.

Meanwhile, Manchester's trade was generally restricted to the import of raw cotton for the Lancashire mills and the subsequent export of textiles. Never able to handle very large tonnages it was nevertheless at one time Britain's third largest port after London and Liverpool. Today little remains of that heritage.

Liverpool had one railway feature that was unique in Britain. As a child I often used to visit my father who was in business in the city and occasionally we travelled on the Liverpool Overhead Railway. Built in 1887 the line ran the length of the docks from Dingle in the south to Seaforth Sands in the north, a distance of around 7 miles, giving unrivalled views from its elevated position of ships being loaded and discharged. To be allowed to travel such a route was a small boy's delight and I recall thinking that its demolition in the 1950s to make way for various road improvement schemes was a major act of vandalism. In its time the line was used to pioneer electric automatic signalling and was the first to use an electric motor coach to haul trailing passenger carriages. Apparently, the elevated railway was always known by Liverpool stevedores as the 'umbi', short for umbrella, since it provided them with a covered passage when walking from one dock to another!

Liverpool lies on the Irish Sea and prior to 1900 there was no major church in the city. Two cathedrals have since been built, an Anglican cathedral begun in 1904 and consecrated in 1978, with its Roman Catholic counterpart being started rather later but completed earlier in 1967. Approaching Liverpool through the city's southern suburbs aboard a train from Manchester Piccadilly, or equally aboard an express from London, and sitting on the left-hand side, the visitor gets an excellent view of both cathedrals across the rooftops of the city about a mile before reaching the tunnels that herald arrival into Lime Street Station. An equally good view can be obtained by travellers from Chester as their

Liverpool Overhead Railway poster. (NRM)

train proceeds up the Wirral Peninsula before crossing beneath the river Mersey into the centre of Liverpool.

The Roman Catholic cathedral was designed by Sir Fredrick Gibberd and is cylindrical in shape, with a conical roof topped by a tapering, coloured glass tower. Sometimes irreverently referred to by local people as 'Paddy's Wigwam' it is situated about half a mile from the Anglican cathedral standing on St James's Mount.

Liverpool Cathedral

A magnificent building in the Gothic style but constructed in the twentieth century, the cathedral took seventy-four years to complete and was finished in 1978. It stands above the city and the river Mersey not far from its Roman Catholic counterpart.

Look for the East and West windows, the War Memorial Chapel in the eastern transept, the Dulverton Bridge and the memorial commemorating the architect's achievement in the central space and climb the tower for wonderful views of the city and its surrounds.

Liverpool Anglican Cathedral is a mile from the centre of the city and dominates all around it. It is the largest cathedral in area in England and the fifth largest in the world. It was built as a modern expression of the medieval style. It is 671 feet long and the central tower, donated by the Vestey family, which had links to the city through shipping, rises to 331 feet. Liverpool has many fine waterfront and city buildings constructed using wealth generated through maritime trade in the eighteenth and nineteenth centuries, but the twentieth-century Anglican cathedral stands comparison with them all.

The new diocese of Liverpool was formed in 1880 when a bishop was appointed. Since he had no cathedral it was decided to build one and, following detailed research and discussion, a competition was held to judge a number of architectural plans. The design by Giles Gilbert Scott was chosen and in 1903 he was commissioned to build a cathedral 'as speedily as possible'. The

The west front of Liverpool Cathedral.

Looking from the top of the tower towards the Roman Catholic cathedral.

Looking from the tower towards the pier head and river Mersey.

The bridge.

early years of construction were marked by disagreement over aspects of the design submitted by Scott. However, following the laying of the foundation stone by Edward VII in July 1904 and after the architect had altered the original plan to build twin towers, replacing them with a single central tower, the work proceeded until completion in 1978. Building was disrupted during both world wars, most seriously in the Second World War when Liverpool and its docks were heavily bombed. Nearly 1,500 people were killed in a raid on the city on one night alone in May 1941, but building never stopped and the tower was completed in 1942. It is testimony to the extraordinary spirit of the people of Liverpool that this happened.

Walking into the cathedral is like entering an enormous cavern. The scale of the interior, its lofty Gothic arches – the largest ever built – and its uncluttered space dwarf the visitor. The red Triassic limestone, which darkens the interior, accentuates the feeling of being in a subterranean grotto. The distance from the high altar to the west end is magnified by the central space and the Dulverton Bridge standing above the nave, which is itself at a lower level than the rest of the building. This lower area is termed the well. Services held using the quire and central space can seat large numbers of people.

When I visited, the quire was being renovated and could not be viewed. However, it was possible to see the high altar and behind it, the reredos, which was built as part of the east wall of the cathedral; it shows the Crucifixion and the Last Supper and above it the East Window reflects the *Te Deum*, that traditional hymn of praise, the opening words of which are: *We praise the, O God, we acknowledge to be the Lord... .* To the south of the quire is the Lady chapel, the first part of the cathedral to be completed, in 1910. The windows were destroyed during the Second World War and have been replaced. The Lady chapel is the size of many parish churches and has its own organ.

Returning to the quire, the organ is one of the most powerful in the world and has nearly 10,000 pipes arrayed both above the quire itself and facing towards the open space. An eastern transept separates the quire from the open space and the northern alcove contains the War Memorial Chapel, dedicated to those from the area who lost their lives in two world wars. HMS *Liverpool's* ship's bell is a reminder of the vital role played by countless servicemen, sailors, stevedores and dockside workers during the Battle of the Atlantic, when the people of Liverpool were very much in the front line in the struggle against Nazi Germany.

Amongst those commemorated in the War Memorial Chapel is Captain Noel Chavasse, the only double Victoria Cross from the First World War and one of only three people to win a bar to his VC since the medal's creation by Queen Victoria. Chavasse was one of the twin sons of Bishop Chavasse, Liverpool's second bishop, who led the work to ensure that the building of the cathedral went on despite problems imposed by war, recession and the continuous need to find the money to bring a project of such a size to fruition. Noel Chavasse, Medical Officer with the local King's Regiment, won his VC and Bar in Flanders in the First World War 'for conspicuous bravery and devotion to duty while under fire'. He was killed in Belgium in 1917, aged thirty-two. His twin brother Christopher was an Army chaplain and later served as Bishop of Rochester.

In the centre of the central space, inlaid in the floor, is a simple memorial commemorating Sir Giles Gilbert Scott, the architect and the inspiration for so much of what was achieved during the building of the cathedral.

HMS *Liverpool's* ship's bell.

The western transept separates the central space from the nave, or well, which is crowned by the Dulverton Bridge at its eastern end. Such a structure must surely be the only feature of its kind in an English cathedral. The word 'nave' derives from the Latin *navis*, meaning ship, and entering it symbolizes a congregation and their priests as passengers sailing together to meet their God. This reference to a ship seems particularly apt at Liverpool given that the nave is lower than the rest of the ground plan of the cathedral.

The tower of the cathedral can be entered from the south side near the bridge and after two lift rides and climbing a further 108 steps, a visitor gets a wonderful view of places around the city; Blackpool Tower to the north; the hills of North Wales to the south-

The Laymen's Window.

west and the two Runcorn bridges to the south, where the main rail and road routes to the city cross the river Mersey from Cheshire. On the ascent to the top of the tower is a chamber housing the cathedral bells, the heaviest of which, *Great George*, weighs 14½ tons and is only tolled on special occasions. A view of the inside of the cathedral showing the nave and central space can be obtained from one of the two chambers passed through on the way up.

The west end was finished after Giles Gilbert Scott's death and for a period there was some doubt as to whether the architect's original plan could be fulfilled as he intended, due to a lack of resources. Roger Pinkney, a pupil of Scott's, was asked to devise an alternative design, which he managed to achieve while still adhering to the architect's original intentions. Encased within the stone work of the west end is the Benedicite Window based on that great canticle that begins: *O all ye works of the Lord, bless ye the Lord* .... At one stage in the construction of the cathedral, stone from the local quarry was in short supply and it was therefore decided to use stone blocks compressed from quarry dust and chippings as an alternative. On hearing of the plan, Lady Royden, the wife of a prominent Liverpool ship owner and politician who was in his time Chairman of Cunard and a director of the LMSR, remarked of the decision, 'God will know!'

On the south side of the nave are two windows, the Parsons' Window and the Laymen's Window. The latter commemorates those involved in the work of construction and those whose generosity made possible the building so masterfully designed and expedited by Giles Gilbert Scott. It gave me enormous pleasure to read the names of my grandparents, John and Magdalene Naylor, in the bottom right-hand corner of the Layman's Window. John Naylor was a Liverpool banker who died in 1906 just as building was starting. His support and that of many others was all important to the success of a project that, although not completed until well into the second Elizabethan age, would have originated in the minds of our Victorian ancestors.

In 2012 I happened to be visiting Napier in New Zealand and went to the cathedral there, which, along with most of the rest of the city, had to be rebuilt following a devastating earthquake in 1931. Archbishop Lesser, who was behind the rebuilding of the cathedral, began his ministry at Liverpool Cathedral. The links between the two churches are marked by two sandstone crosses made of the same stone as that used at Liverpool, one being presented at the time of the dedication and the other when the new building was consecrated. Both are in the nave at Napier.

Everything about Liverpool Cathedral is on a grand scale. The height of the central tower and the building's internal arches, the length of the cathedral, the concept of a bridge astride the eastern end of the nave and the unfussy nature of the interior, with few memorials or tombs, all give the building a dignified if somewhat austere feel. Built by men of purpose it symbolizes the spirit of Liverpool, a city that has had to contend with and overcome many challenges in its long life and today delights in the presence of two magnificent twentieth-century cathedrals within its boundaries.

North

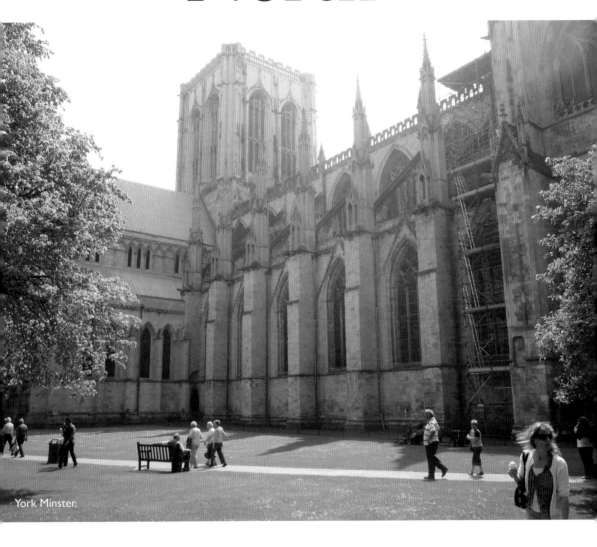

York Minster.

Chapter 13

York

Getting There

York is less than two hours from King's Cross by a fast train. Passengers have a choice of carrier, there currently being more than one service provider on the route. Situated on the main East Coast line to Scotland, the city also has excellent connections to Newcastle, Edinburgh and Glasgow.

Other services connect to Leeds, Manchester and the Midlands.

Railway Notes

George Hudson, a nineteenth-century pioneer railway builder, was born at Howsham near York. His mercurial career as a railway developer, financial entrepreneur, three times Lord Mayor of the city and MP for Sunderland for fourteen years, spanned seventy years and his achievements, particularly those connected with the boom years of railway construction in the 1800s, are well documented. Such was the nature of the man that he never rested on his laurels, always endeavouring to be engaged in a fresh venture, until he was finally ruined by financial scandal and died in penury. A draper by profession he is today recalled as one of York's more famous citizens and is remembered in a street that bears his name, and a portrait in the Mansion House. Hudson may not rank alongside the Stephensons, Brunel or Telford as an engineer but he was certainly their equal in financing and promoting many schemes during the years of railway construction in Britain. He was not known as the 'Railway King' for nothing.

York has long been associated with railways. It can be numbered alongside Crewe, Swindon, Eastleigh, Derby, Doncaster and Darlington as places where locomotives or rolling stock were built in the nineteenth and twentieth centuries. Today carriage building no longer takes place in York and much of the land once used for marshalling yards and sidings has been put to other uses. However, the connection to railways is still there in the form of the magnificent National Railway Museum. Opened in 1975 and housed in a building close to the station the museum contains exhibits of locomotives, carriages, goods wagons, royal trains and signalling equipment along with comprehensive explanations of how railways have been developed and operated over two centuries. Prior to the museum's establishment the big four railway companies had assembled their own railway-related material, much of which is now on display at York. The museum sets out not just to explain past developments but also seeks to show how railways have changed the world. Given time it is to be hoped the NRM might one day spearhead exploration as to how best to develop railway technology to meet future transport needs.

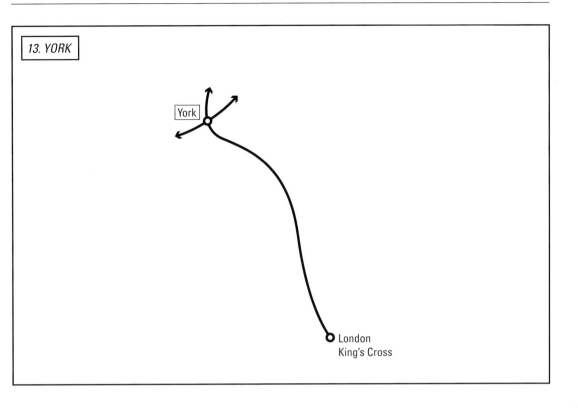

A High Speed Train about to depart York for Scotland.

A selection of NRM exhibits.

York Minster

The great minster, the fourth on the site, started in 1220 and finished in 1472, is England's largest Gothic church. It has been ravaged by three disastrous fires in the last 200 years.

Look for the minster's four great windows, the quire screen with its fifteen kings of England from 1066 to 1461, Archbishop Lamplugh's statue in the south quire aisle and St Nicholas's Chapel and its *Twelve days of Christmas* kneelers.

York Minster is the largest Gothic cathedral north of the Alps and has the widest nave of any cathedral in England. Its vast, uncluttered, light interior immediately strikes visitors as they survey the loftiness of its quire, nave and transepts. Completed in 1472, the present minster is believed to be the fourth cathedral to be built in York. Its immediate predecessor was constructed by the Normans at the end of the eleventh century while the present structure was built over it starting in 1220. To build a cathedral must have been challenge enough for York's medieval masons and carpenters but to do so while at the same time demolishing a previous building seems incredible. As a result it is possible that the pillars in the present minster may be filled with rubble from the Norman cathedral.

The west front.

The location of the first and second minsters is not known but they are believed to have been situated in the vicinity of the present cathedral. The first church, built by Edwin, the Saxon King of Northumbria in 627, for his own baptism by Bishop Paulinus, was a wooden structure, later thought to have been augmented by a second, more permanent building on the same site. Both churches and other buildings connected with the early Church in York would have suffered at the hands of invaders, principally the Saxons and the Vikings. Much later, William the Conqueror came north after the Norman invasion of 1066 to destroy the city before directing Thomas, the Bishop of Bayeux and probably the first Archbishop of York, to build a cathedral capable of symbolizing Norman power and permanence. Thomas completed his task remarkably quickly and is also credited with setting down the rules and procedures for the governance of cathedrals. Many of these rules are embodied in practices still followed by cathedral chapters.

One of the glories of York is its stained glass. The four great windows of the minster – the East and West windows, the Five Sisters Window in the north transept and the Rose Window in the south transept – were all built between the thirteenth and fifteenth centuries. In total there are 128 windows in the building, all of which will probably have at some stage been removed for restoration. The never-ending work of maintaining the minster in good order could not be better illustrated than by the current programme to completely refurbish the stonework of the east end and the glass of the East Window. If laid flat on the ground that window would fill an area

The quire screen showing the first seven of fifteen kings of England whose combined rule covered 395 years.

The quire and high altar.

The nave following the Maundy service in 2012.

the size of a tennis court. Painted between 1405 and 1408 by John Thornton of Coventry, it was commissioned and paid for by Bishop Skirlaugh of Durham. In its upper twenty-seven panels the window tells the story of the Creation as recounted in the Book of Genesis, while those below predict the end of the world as envisaged in the Book of Revelation of St John the Divine, the last book of the Bible.

The other three main windows all reward study. The West Window donated by Archbishop Melton in 1338 depicts archbishops and the apostles in its lower panels and events in the life of Christ towards the top. The Five Sisters Window, with its thirteenth-century grisaille glass shaped in abstract patterns, and the Rose Window, the glass of which celebrates the end of the War of the Roses in 1485, are treasures of which the minster is rightly proud. Each reflects an architectural period of the building's construction, which broadly spanned 250 years. St William's Window, also painted by John Thornton, in the north quire aisle, and the superb Jesse Window on the south side of the nave are both deserving of scrutiny; however, use of a pair of binoculars is advised.

Even during its construction, York Minster suffered disaster. In 1407 the vast central tower collapsed and had to be rebuilt. The cause was probably the weight of the tower built upon unstable ground. That the previous Norman minster was built on a raft of oak tree trunks lends substance to this supposition. The tower was subsequently rebuilt, plans for a spire being abandoned and a lantern tower substituted. The problem of potential collapse again manifested itself in 1967, when the minster authorities were warned that cracks appearing in the building's fabric were a cause for concern. The decision was therefore made to excavate the area beneath the tower to a depth of several feet and to underpin the four supporting pillars using concrete, reinforced with steel rods, resulting in the stabilization of the structure. Hopefully the danger of subsidence has now been eliminated.

The minster suffered little damage during either Henry VIII's reign or the Civil War of the seventeenth century when Sir Thomas Fairfax decreed that the building should not be looted by the victorious Roundheads following their victory at Marston Moor in 1644, a battle that effectively brought the Civil War to an end and sealed the fate of Charles I.

However, the greatest challenge faced by the minster in its long history has been the damage inflicted by a succession of fires. Within the last 200 years, three serious conflagrations have occurred, all resulting in the need for major restoration work. The first in 1829 was caused by arson when a malcontent, Jonathon Martin, deliberately started a fire in the quire, destroying the stalls, organ and a large area of the roof. Martin was put on trial but was found to be mentally deficient. Eleven years later, in 1840, negligence by a workman, who left a candle burning in the roof space, led to the destruction of the nave roof timbers and the collapse of the minster bells. On that occasion the Lord Mayor of York had to send to Leeds for additional fire-fighting resources, which arrived by train.

The most recent fire was that of July 1984, when the roof of the south transept was set alight by lightning or some other electrical activity in the atmosphere. The resultant fire raged for several

The Great West Window.

hours until the Fire Brigade managed to collapse the still un-burnt timbers of the transept roof into the space below, thereby isolating the seat of the fire. Had such action not been taken it is possible that the whole minster might have been destroyed. Four years later, the transept was fully refurbished with the Rose Window, which had shattered into 40,000 pieces, repaired and reset and the roof and its bosses rebuilt. Six of the new bosses depict events of the twentieth century and, following publicity on the BBC's *Blue Peter* TV programme inviting children to contribute ideas, the six were chosen from 32,000 entries. They depict such diverse events as the fire itself, space travel, the Moon Landing of 1968, world famine, the raising of the medieval warship the *Mary Rose* in 1982 and exploration of the depths of the oceans.

One of the minster's most admired monuments is the quire screen, or *pulpitum*, which separates the nave from the quire. Built in the fifteenth century it is carved with statues of the fifteen kings of England who ruled from 1066 to 1461. An anomaly in construction led to the centre line of the quire and the centre line of the nave not being precisely aligned. There is a mismatch of 2 or 3 degrees, with the centre line of the quire lying slightly to the north of that of the nave. This probably arose from Archbishop Walter de Grey's original decision, when planning his Gothic cathedral, to retain the Norman quire built by Thomas, and to connect it in due course to the new building, a decision later rescinded when it was instead decided to rebuild the quire. For a variety of reasons medieval architects had difficulty in aligning the two main parts of the minster.

There are several monuments to archbishops and others in the aisles surrounding the quire. One in the south aisle, a statue of Thomas Lamplugh, archbishop for two years until 1691, shows him with two right feet. Lamplugh was generally a supporter of the Catholic faith and an adherent of James II. When the Protestant William of Orange arrived in Britain and ousted James from the throne, Lamplugh, already the archbishop, quickly paid homage to the new monarch. His propensity 'to blow with the wind' gained him a reputation as a veritable Vicar of Bray. Whether his two right feet arose from his practice of changing position to suit the views of his superiors or because shoes in the seventeenth century were generally made of one pattern and therefore interchangeable between feet, or even because the carving of his statue was left to an unsupervised apprentice, we shall never know. See Chapter 6 for William of Orange's sojourn in Exeter Cathedral, where Thomas Lamplugh had previously been the bishop and where William stopped on his way to London.

The minster is the seat of the Archbishop of York, second only to the Archbishop of Canterbury in seniority in the Church of England. This relationship is reflected in their respective titles, by which York is designated 'Primate of England' while Canterbury is 'the Primate of all England'; this distinction is further emphasized by the division of their responsibilities, which allocates the supervision of the fourteen North of England dioceses to the Archbishop of York while his senior colleague is responsible for the other thirty. However, it was not always such a harmonious relationship. Up until the middle of the fourteenth century no clear direction was given by the Pope as to which archbishop was the senior and in medieval times this regularly led to a series of protracted disputes, sometimes culminating in violence between the supporters of the two primates. Matters were brought to a head in the fourteenth century when Archbishop John Thoresby of York, nicknamed the 'peace-maker', proposed in 1352 a compromise that reflected the archbishops' separate but interlocking responsibilities, an arrangement that endures to this day. *See also* Chapter 1 for other details of the two primates.

Chapter 14

Carlisle

■ The Settle-Carlisle Railway ■ **Carlisle Cathedral** ■ a valiant chaplain ■

Getting There

Most express services from London to Scotland along the West Coast route call at Carlisle, the last station in England before crossing the border. Pendolino trains leave from Euston Station and take three-and-a-half hours to reach the border city. This is the most direct route.

Carlisle is also connected to a number of other centres by rail. Leeds is three hours away travelling via the Settle-Carlisle route and Newcastle an hour by the line that follows the river Tyne valley from the east.

An alternative route from London would be to travel to Newcastle along the East Coast route and to then take the Tyne Valley line.

Railway Notes

The West Coast route from London to Scotland has been comprehensively upgraded over the last ten years and in its present state probably represents the limit to which a railway built in the Victorian era can be further engineered to achieve even higher speeds and reliability without causing very considerable disruption. For this reason attention is now turning to the building of a completely new 'state of the art' high-speed railway capable of speeds in excess of 250 miles per hour, something already being achieved in other parts of the world. Chapter 1 considered the creation of the High Speed One route from the Continent to London and, in due course, its counterpart, High Speed Two, may be built northwards from London, thereby connecting the most important centres of population within Britain to the capital and Europe. Carlisle could eventually be situated on that line. Meanwhile, today the city can be reached by trains from a number of directions, the most interesting route historically being the railway across the spine of the Pennines from Leeds to the south.

No railway in Britain better illustrates the challenges and hardships the early railway pioneers faced than does the 72 miles of railway that links Settle in North Yorkshire with Carlisle. The building of the line through some of the most inhospitable and isolated terrain in the North of England demanded great tenacity and physical courage and symbolizes all that seems most admirable about our Victorian ancestors and their determination to succeed, come what may. Whether the line was ever strictly necessary has long been a matter for debate and it would certainly not be built today. Its justification as an operational railway still attracts criticism, but its retention as part of the national network now appears more assured providing as it does both a third route to Scotland and improved local access.

Much has been written in recent times about the line and the campaign of the 1970s and 1980s to ensure its continued use despite British Rail's attempts to run it down and then make a case

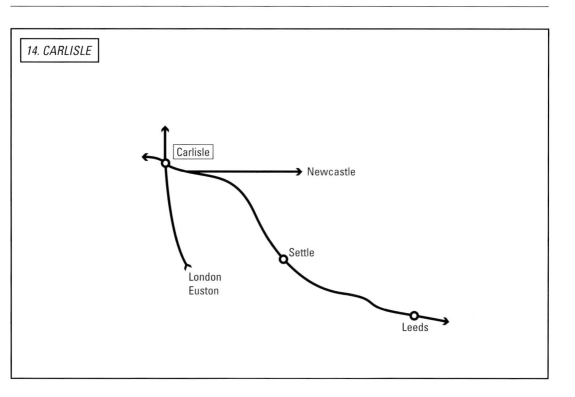

14. CARLISLE

Carlisle

Newcastle

Settle

London
Euston

Leeds

The southbound Cumbrian Mountain Express approaching Ais Gill.

Ribblehead Viaduct.

for its closure on economic grounds. However, in 1989 a reprieve was granted when widespread public support eventually forced British Rail to abandon its plans. Today the line, extensively improved and with its stations lovingly looked after by volunteers from the Friends of the Settle-Carlisle Line, carries a mix of passenger services, freight trains and excursions. Many of the latter are steam-hauled by locomotives that regularly travelled the line more than fifty years ago.

The country north of Settle is breathtaking. Climbing almost continuously for 22 miles at a ruling gradient of 1 foot in every 100 feet for much of the way from Settle Junction to its Pennine summit at Ais Gill, at 1,169 feet the highest railway summit in England, the line passes across rough moorland bisected by deep valleys. For much of its journey the passage of a train is dominated by the high mountain peaks of the Pennines, amongst them Ingleborough and Pen-y-ghent. Tunnels abound and there are twenty-two viaducts, all built by navvies in the 1870s at a considerable cost in lives.

The best-known viaduct is that at Ribblehead built to carry the line over Batty Moss, a large area of low-lying wet ground. The viaduct has twenty-four arches all over 100 feet high. A couple of miles to the north is the longest tunnel on the route at Blea Moor, nearly 2 miles in length; at one stage in the construction of the permanent way more than 6,000 men were based in the area of Ribblehead and Blea Moor to build these two structures, most of them living under appalling conditions. Some remains of their campsites and the tracks and tramways they used at Ribblehead can still be seen.

The climb northwards from Settle to Ais Gill was known by enginemen as the 'Long Drag'. Hauling a heavily laden train of several hundred tons could take its toll of a steam locomotive and

Coal from Scotland crossing Ribblehead Viaduct.

as a result many trains had to be double-headed by the addition of a second locomotive or pushed from in rear; it required considerable skill by engine crews to conduct their trains over such a mountainous route. Today modern diesel units make light work of the gradients, although when I last travelled the line on a northbound train the driver was pushing his train hard for most of the climb to the summit.

Weather has always added to the many other hazards of negotiating the line over the Pennines. Wind, the ferocity of which could slow even the most powerful of locomotives, and snow are amongst the worst of the elements with which drivers have always had to contend. There are countless tales of trains lost in snowdrifts while extreme weather conditions have sometimes led to an increased risk of human error. It is easy to imagine how an overworked signalman, isolated in his signal box and agitated by the wind and the weather outside, might suffer a temporary lapse of memory and make a fatal error. This happened in the early hours of Christmas Eve 1910, when the signalman at Hawes Junction, now Garsdale, allowed the overnight sleeping car express from London to Scotland onto the line to Carlisle having just dispatched two light engines in the same direction. It did not take the express long to catch up and run into the two engines and nine people perished in the ensuing fire.

The campaign to save the line from closure was as much emotional as practical. When built it gave the Midland Railway access to Scotland without the need to share the routes of either of its two competitors, the London, Midland and Scottish Railway to the west or the London & North Eastern Railway to the east. Never as popular as its East and West coast rivals, the Midland Railway's heyday came in the years before the First World War when, amongst other services, it

A diesel train leaving Blea Moor Tunnel.

operated expresses from St Pancras to Scotland. However, after 1945 the line gradually slipped into decline. The decision forty years later to retain it is beginning to prove commercially justified and may become more so as the ramifications of global warming become clearer. Only time will tell whether the railway will still be operating in 150 years time or whether the building of a high-speed route to the north will lead to renewed pressure for it to be closed.

A local train at Garsdale.

Carlisle Cathedral

The cathedral of one of the oldest and most northerly English dioceses, it lies only a few miles south of the border with Scotland and dates from 1122.

Look for the remaining bays of the Norman nave, the memorial to The Reverend Theodore Bayly Hardy, the Brougham Triptych in St Wilfrid's Chapel and the glorious painted barrel ceiling of the quire.

After passing the summit of the line at Ais Gill a northbound train runs quickly down the river Eden valley to Carlisle. First developed in Roman times the city has experienced many upheavals in its long history, having always been 'in the front line' during centuries of warfare between English and Scottish rulers. Hadrian's Wall, built by the Roman emperor of that name in 128, was intended to protect Roman Britain from the Scots. It runs for 73 miles from the North Sea to the Solway Firth and ends to the west of the city when it reaches the waters of the firth.

At the time of the Norman Conquest Carlisle was part of Scotland, the city not being reincorporated into England by William II until 1092. Little is known of any early churches in the

The east end of Carlisle Cathedral.

area although the discovery of various remains indicates their existence prior to the arrival of the Normans. In 1122 Henry I gave permission for the founding of an Augustinian priory, dedicated to St Mary, and eleven years later the priory church was designated as the cathedral to serve the newly established diocese of Carlisle. Today's cathedral is the second smallest in England, the seat of a bishop whose large diocese was carved out of Durham in 1133. Following the establishment of the cathedral, St Mary's Church continued to be part of the building and parish services were held in the nave. The priory was dissolved on the orders of Henry VIII in 1540. In the meantime the cathedral suffered fire damage in 1292 and the collapse of its Norman tower in 1380.

Built of sandstone, the interior of the cathedral is somewhat dark. The nave was originally much longer than it is today; cut back between 1649 and 1652 during the Civil War, it now consists of a single bay, which, since 1949, has become a military chapel, originally that of the Border Regiment and today that of its successor, the Duke of Lancaster's Regiment. Sir Walter Scott was married in the nave in 1797.

Close by on the north side of the cathedral is a memorial to a remarkable man. Reverend Theodore Bayly Hardy was a chaplain in the First World War. During the course of three years' service in the trenches his many acts of unselfish heroism and his unfailing dedication to his fellow men earned him awards of the Military Cross, the Distinguished Service Order and Victoria Cross. He was the most highly decorated non-combatant of the war. He died of wounds three weeks before the Armistice in 1918. Prior to enlistment at the age of fifty-one he had served both as a schoolmaster and later as the incumbent at Hutton Roof near Kirby Lonsdale. His story, written in the book *Its Only Me* by David Raw, tells of the life of a chaplain in the trenches who experienced the full horrors and suffering of the Great War. Raw's account of Hardy's life is profoundly moving. A friend and close colleague of Hardy's from the Great War, Reverend Geoffrey Studdert Kennedy, is similarly remembered in a window of Worcester Cathedral, mentioned in Chapter 9.

St Wilfrid's Chapel in the north transept is used for weekday Eucharistic services and behind the altar is the Brougham Triptych, carved in Antwerp in the early sixteenth century and brought to Carlisle by the then Lord Chancellor,

The north transept.

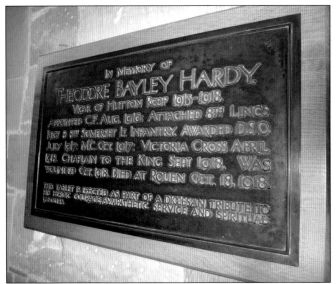

Memorial to the Reverend Theodore Bayley Hardy in Carlisle Cathedral.

Lord Brougham. It is on loan to the cathedral.

The quire contains the fifteenth-century canons' stalls, underneath the seats of which are carved misericords that allowed the early occupants to perch, thereby surreptitiously resting their limbs when required to stand for long periods during worship. As in many cathedrals the stalls are allocated to the dean and his chapter colleagues, the honorary canons of Carlisle and the principal civil dignitaries in the county. The glorious painted barrel ceiling of the quire is medieval and was restored to its original state by Owen Jones in 1856 and again repainted in 1970. The tops of the pillars in the presbytery to the east are carved with illustrations depicting the work of the medieval farmer. Each month records a different activity; in March he is seen pruning his vines while September records the harvesting of the grapes.

The East Window contains some important fourteenth-century glass while the tracery is thought to be the work of Ivo de Raughton, who did similar work in York Minster and at Selby Abbey. The top of the window is medieval and depicts the Last Judgement. Christ shows the righteous to Paradise while the wicked are condemned to eternal damnation. The lower part of the window shows scenes from the life of Christ and dates from 1861.

Carlisle Cathedral may be small but it is important as the centre of a large, rural diocese and symbolizes for the people of Cumbria a close attachment to their bishop and their county. It may not be as well known or as well visited as some English cathedrals but at least one of its deans achieved the highest office in the nineteenth century: Dean Archibald Campbell Tait, who was at Carlisle from 1849 when he completed a major restoration of the cathedral, subsequently became Bishop of London and then Archbishop of Canterbury, dying in 1882. His tomb is in the north-east transept of Canterbury Cathedral. On a more sombre note, the main window in St Wilfrid's Chapel in Carlisle commemorates his five daughters, all of whom died of scarlet fever over a period of six weeks in 1856.

Carlisle is well worth a visit. While the journey to reach it travelling by the Settle-Carlisle route may not be the fastest or most convenient way to get to the city from the south, the journey across the Pennines is a must for anyone interested in Britain's railway heritage. The grandeur of the scenery, the scale of the original undertaking and the commitment to build a railway across such desolate terrain can but impress even the most hardened of travellers.

Chapter 15

Newcastle and Durham

■ Fast running in pre-war years ■ the Stockton & Darlington Railway ■ **Newcastle Cathedral**
■ **Durham Cathedral** ■ St Cuthbert ■ the Prince Bishops ■ the Venerable Bede ■

Getting There

An express from King's Cross takes just over two-and-a-half hours to reach Durham and a further twenty minutes to Newcastle. Most, but not all, East Coast services call at Durham en route to Newcastle. A carefully planned visit to both cathedrals is possible in one day from London.

Railway Notes

North of York, the East Coast Main Line from London runs almost straight for 40 miles until it reaches a few miles south of Darlington. Quadrupled in the early years of the twentieth century to provide scope for the running of faster and more frequent trains, the stretch of line gained a reputation for the regular achievement of speeds of up to 100 miles an hour by steam engines. Expresses of the inter-war years – like the *Flying Scotsman* hauled by powerful, streamlined locomotives designed by Sir Nigel Gresley, the Chief Mechanical Engineer of the London & North Eastern Railway – travelled from London to Edinburgh in little more than six hours, often without stopping. Troughs laid between the rails allowed a locomotive's water supply to be replenished without the need for a stop by the simple expedient of lowering a scoop beneath a locomotive's tender into a metal water channel between the running rails. Equally, a change of engine crews could be undertaken on the move by the construction of a narrow corridor within a locomotive's tender to enable a relief crew to walk through from the train while the latter was in motion. Today's high-speed trains and their

Flying Scotsman poster. (NRM)

158

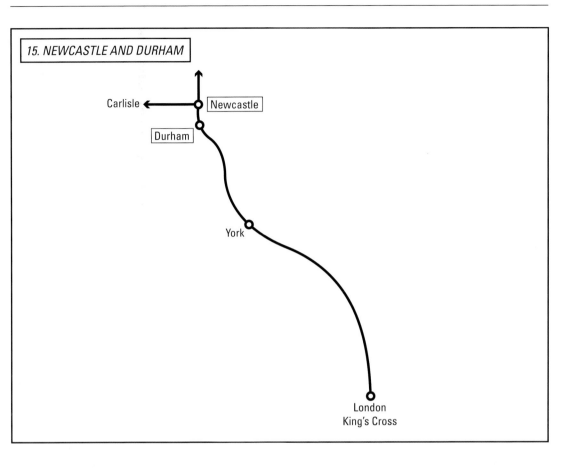

15. NEWCASTLE AND DURHAM

Carlisle ← Newcastle

Durham

York

London
King's Cross

The Tyne bridges, Newcastle.

electric equivalents may complete the journey to Edinburgh in around four-and-a-half hours, but they will never be able reproduce quite the same glamour or sense of excitement regularly achieved by steam-hauled expresses in their heyday.

In its day, Darlington, approximately halfway between York and Newcastle, was another major railway centre where workshops once built locomotives and rolling stock. However, the town is best remembered as the place where George Stephenson's locomotive, *Locomotion*, hauled carriages on the world's first public railway in 1825 from Shildon to Darlington and thence to Stockton. Like the Liverpool & Manchester Railway the name of the Stockton & Darlington is synonymous with Britain's Victorian engineers' achievement in developing the world's first railways. Shildon today houses an extension of York's National Railway Museum and there is a fine exhibition of rolling stock and railway memorabilia at the station. Meanwhile, there is a working replica of *Locomotion* at the Beamish Museum in County Durham.

The East Coast main line north of York.

Newcastle Cathedral

An ancient parish church, which only became a cathedral in 1882. It is surmounted by a rare 'crown spire' dating from the end of the fifteenth century.

Look for the statue of St Nicholas on the baptistry screen, the font, the depiction of famous local men in the windows of St George's Chapel and the reredos behind the high altar.

The Church of St Nicholas in Newcastle only became a cathedral in July 1882 when the new diocese of Newcastle was created out of that of Durham. Growing industrialization in North East England and population expansion made such a separation necessary. An earlier plan to create a city based upon Newcastle and Gateshead and to create a bishopric in 1553, had foundered when Queen Mary refused to allow the planned legislation to be enacted.

St Nicholas's had no monastic foundation and for most of its existence has been the parish church of the city. A wooden building was erected on the site of the present cathedral towards the end of the eleventh century and this was replaced by a stone structure a hundred years later. Further development then took place up to the fifteenth century, when the tower and its crown were added. Today the cathedral stands close to the city centre, isolated by two main streets, and only a few hundred yards from the railway station and the magnificent series of bridges spanning the river Tyne.

St Nicholas, a bishop of the fourth century, is the patron saint of mariners and children and is depicted in several windows and carvings throughout the cathedral. Immediately inside the west end is the baptistry and its fifteenth-century limestone font with positioned above it a finely carved wooden canopy. The font was thought to be in danger of being destroyed at the time of the Civil War in the mid-seventeenth century but a local mason dismantled and hid it until the restoration of the monarchy in 1660.

When the church became the seat of the bishop its interior was adjusted to reflect its new status as his cathedral. Much work was devoted to refitting the quire and the

The crown spire of Newcastle Cathedral.

dean and canons' stalls while an appropriate *cathedra* and the rood screen separating the quire from the nave, and a new pulpit were all built. The work was designed by a local architect, Robert Johnson, and the screen carved by Ralph Hedley, who had a workshop in the city. Further east is the high altar with a towering reredos, or screen, behind, partly hiding the view of the East Window. The reredos is carved with figures of saints and angels and low down on the north side of the screen is a statue of Arthur Thomas Lloyd, the first vicar of Newcastle following the granting of cathedral status in 1882. He later returned as the third bishop of the diocese in 1903.

Newcastle's close links to the sea, ship building and Scandinavia are evident throughout the building. Admiral Collingwood, Lord Nelson's deputy and eventual successor in command when the latter was shot at the Battle of Trafalgar in 1805, is commemorated by a bust near the north door. St George's Chapel contains windows honouring some of Tyneside's entrepreneurs, men such as Andrew Laing and Charles Parsons, who established many of the area's great industrial and marine enterprises. Parsons developed the

The window commemorating St Edmund, King Edward the Confessor and Lord Stamfordham in Newcastle Cathedral.

first steam turbine in 1884. Ten years later he built an experimental turbine-driven yacht, the *Turbinia*, which was demonstrated at the Spithead Review in 1897. My great-uncle, Christopher Leyland, an associate of Charles Parsons, helped in these enterprises. An image of *Turbinia* is shown in one of the windows in the chapel. Also shown in the same chapel are windows recording the achievements of Lord Stamfordham, private secretary and wise counsellor to Queen Victoria and George V, and Lord Grey, the Foreign Secretary of the same era and later founder of the Royal Society for the Protection of Birds. Both were local men of renown.

Beneath the quire on the north side is the Crypt Chapel, originally a fourteenth-century charnel house used for the storage of bones when the churchyard became full. Although much altered in the nineteenth century when promoted to cathedral status, St Nicholas's still reflects the features of a parish church. Its simple, unpretentious style somehow seems appropriate in a city where the proud Geordie people get on with life regardless of what may be happening elsewhere in the world.

Durham Cathedral

A cathedral whose bishops once ruled as princes.

Look for St Cuthbert's shrine, the Norman pillars of the nave, the Galilee Chapel and the Chapel of Nine Altars. Climb the central tower to understand the size and grandeur of the cathedral.

Ajourney of no more than twenty minutes from Newcastle brings the traveller south to Durham. The cathedral stands on a rocky promontory high above a loop of the river Wear, alongside the city's Norman castle and its ancient university. The cathedral provides a magnificent spectacle, especially when approached by train from the south. Its outline dominates the city while the interior of the building gives an impression of simple austerity, not inappropriate considering the site's original occupation by humble Benedictine monks a thousand years ago. The contrast with neighbouring Newcastle Cathedral could not be more pronounced.

The origins of a religious settlement in Durham go back many years to the seventh century when St Cuthbert, a monk and later bishop of the monastic community of Lindisfarne on the Northumberland coast, died in 687. Just over 300 years later, having been forced to flee Lindisfarne

The tower of Durham Cathedral.

The tower and north transept.

by Viking raiders and after travelling around Northern England and Southern Scotland from one resting place to another, a party of monks carrying Cuthbert's remains eventually arrived at Durham in 995. The monks wanted a site that would be safe from Viking raiders and they built a small wooden church to house the saint's relics. Cuthbert, a man of great humility and learning, renowned for his preaching of the Christian gospels throughout the north, soon became a legend, with much of his life's work recorded in the *Lindisfarne Gospels* written in the eighth century. The arrival of Cuthbert's remains on the site of the present-day cathedral later led to the foundation of a Saxon church before a Norman cathedral was begun by Bishop William of Calais in 1093. Apart from the tower, the Galilee Chapel and the Chapel of the Nine Altars, most of the existing cathedral was completed by 1133, a remarkable achievement.

Today St Cuthbert's shrine lies at the eastern end of the cathedral behind the high altar. It is a simple place reached by steps, with the saint's final resting place marked by a plain stone slab upon which is engraved the single Latin word *Cuthbertus*. The shrine was destroyed during the Reformation in 1537 and the precious metals and jewels surrounding it removed; the coffin was re-interred after it had been opened and found to contain remains clothed in a priest's vestments.

Much earlier, in 1104, when Cuthbert's remains were first placed in the cathedral, there had been found in the coffin a bible believed to have been that of the saint. The seventh-century manuscript, a copy of St John's Gospel, was buried with him when he was originally interred at Lindisfarne and is believed to be the oldest book in Europe. For many years it was kept at Durham but later passed into private hands. More recently it has been on display at the British Museum, which, following a successful appeal in April 2012, purchased it for the nation. Meanwhile, the shrine has been opened on two other occasions and artefacts relevant to St Cuthbert's time placed in a museum in the cloisters.

Sir Walter Scott described Durham Cathedral as 'half church of God, half castle 'gainst the Scots', a phrase that reflected the wish of the Norman kings to demonstrate to the Scots and any invaders from across the North Sea that they had by the end of the eleventh century firmly established themselves as the new rulers of Britain. This expression of intended permanence is reinforced by the size and grandeur of the nave with its huge pillars arranged in pairs, some carved in the Romanesque style with chevron patterns, while others are fluted or sculpted with different geometrical decorations. The pillars and the height of the nave with its three storeys reinforces the immediate impression that the cathedral was built both as a symbol of Norman power and as an expression of a deep Christian faith.

The early years of the Norman dynasty were marked by a succession of raids across the border between England and Scotland. In order to ensure some semblance of control over incursions by the Scots, William the Conqueror and his son William II concluded agreements with the earls of Northumberland and later the bishops at Durham, by which they would rule over a 'buffer zone' south of the river Tyne. This resulted in the bishops being granted self-governing powers to control the area on behalf of the monarch, based many miles to their south. Awarded the title of Prince Bishops they were allowed to hold their own parliament, raise taxes and administer the law, making them amongst the most powerful of medieval rulers of the time. These secular powers gradually fell out of use, finally reverting to the Crown in 1836. The last holder was Bishop William van Mildert, co-founder of Durham University, whose statue is in the Chapel of Nine Altars.

Beyond the nave is the central tower, completed in the Perpendicular style in 1470 and the final part of the cathedral to be built. It rises to a height 218 feet and from the top offers a spectacular view of the surrounding city and the meandering river Wear.

The nave.

Either side of the tower are the two transepts extending sideways from the main body of the cathedral, housing in the south transept a medieval clock built by Prior Castell during the sixteenth century and recently renovated as a working model. Also located in the transept are the regimental chapel of the Durham Light Infantry and a ceremonial banner from the miners' lodge at nearby Haswell Colliery. Both reflect the importance of the links, established over many years, between the regiment, the miners and the cathedral. The Durham coalfield once constituted the area's principal industry while during its time the regiment established an enviable reputation as a superb fighting force. As many as 12,600 of its soldiers died during the First World War, with many others wounded; hardly a family in the county was unaffected. The chapel was dedicated in 1923.

The entrance to the quire was once adorned with an organ screen, which was removed in the nineteenth century to open up the internal view to the east. In retrospect this measure came to be seen as unsuccessful since it created an impression of a tunnel when the length of the cathedral was viewed from the west end. To counteract this effect a Victorian screen and pulpit designed by George Gilbert Scott were installed in 1876. The official cathedral guide, however, questions the appropriateness of 'this sumptuous marble screen in a sandstone building' and also the building of the pulpit carried out at the same time.

The Neville Screen behind the high altar in the sanctuary was completed in 1380. It contains a number of empty niches where formerly there might have been statues of angels and saints. These were taken out at the time of the Reformation and, although probably hidden rather than

The west front.

View from the tower looking west towards the river Wear.

destroyed, their whereabouts remain a mystery. On the south side of the quire is an imposing elevated platform upon which rests the bishop's highly decorated *cathedra*, designed by Bishop Hatfield in the fourteenth century. Beyond the screen is St Cuthbert's shrine and further east the Chapel of Nine Altars, which dates from around 1280.

The chapel was built to accommodate the many pilgrims who came to pray at St Cuthbert's shrine and the altars were originally positioned along the eastern wall, mass being celebrated at one of the altars each day. One of the saints commemorated is St Margaret of Scotland, details of whose life are given in Chapter 5 on Salisbury Cathedral. Bishop Richard Poore, who began the building of the cathedral at Salisbury in 1220, was later translated to Durham, where he supervised the construction of the Chapel of Nine Altars. As a result the original cathedral apse was removed and the eastern end of the cathedral reconstructed in the Early English style, a style followed when Bishop Poore began the building of Salisbury. A large rose window surmounts the chapel.

At the western end of the cathedral is the Galilee Chapel, begun in 1170 and intended as a Lady chapel. The original plan had been to build the chapel at the east end of the cathedral but it collapsed soon after completion, as a result of which Bishop Hugh Le Puiset instead opted to build to the west. Lady chapels are dedicated to the Virgin Mary and are built to the east of the high altar in a cathedral although there are exceptions such as at Ely, where the Lady chapel is separate from the cathedral and located to its north-east.

The Norman Galilee Chapel became a place where worshippers assembled prior to and dispersed after services. As the cathedral guide again explains, 'Galilee was the homeland of Christ from where he "went up" to Jerusalem, so the Galilee Chapel was a place of arrival from which to enter the main cathedral. But Galilee was also where the risen Jesus promised to go ahead of the disciples to meet them. So the Galilee Chapel was also a place of departure and dismissal … .' Within the chapel there lies a tomb that contains the bones of the Venerable Bede, whose writings and recording of history have told us so much about the Saxon church and the life and teachings of St Cuthbert. Bede lived from 673 to 735 and spent nearly all his life in a monastery at Jarrow, a short distance to the north-east of Durham close to the south bank of the river Tyne. The chapel contains several medieval paintings including pictures believed to be of St Cuthbert and St Oswald, ruler of Northumbria.

Durham has always been a place of pilgrimage on account of its close association with the Celtic saints such as Cuthbert, Aidan, Oswald, Hilda and the Venerable Bede. Until the martyrdom of Thomas Becket it was probably even more visited than Canterbury Cathedral. Durham's thousand years of history, the magnificence of its construction and its imposing position high above the city combine to make it one of England's finest cathedrals, a place that should certainly be on any traveller's itinerary.

A freight train on the East Coast mainline.

Chapter 16

Ripon

■ Dr Beeching's 1960s' review of the railway network ■ privatization ■
■ **Ripon Cathedral** ■ Fountains Abbey ■

Getting There

Ripon cannot be reached by rail. However, a train from King's Cross to York takes two hours, followed by a change into a local service and a further twenty-minute journey to reach Thirsk. Thereafter you should use a bus or taxi to Ripon. Total time from London is between three and four hours depending upon the ease of the connections.

An alternative option is to travel by train from London to Harrogate via a change of trains in Leeds and to then take a bus or taxi to Ripon. This is, however, a slower route than via York.

Railway Notes

Less than fifty years ago Britain's railway network covered more than 18,000 miles of track and sidings and reached virtually every corner of the country. In the early 1960s the Government, intent upon cutting the cost of the railways, commissioned Dr Richard Beeching, an eminent scientist, to review the extent and utility of the network, which had remained virtually unchanged since its grouping into four big companies in 1923. When published, Beeching's recommendations envisaged sweeping reductions in the number of routes and stations, particularly in more rural areas. Inter alia, he advocated the complete withdrawal of services on some routes in Scotland, Wales and in the West of England and their replacement with buses. Increased road building was also advocated. The logic underpinning the report was that the railways had become too expensive and incapable of covering their costs, underutilized, inefficient unless modernized and increasingly less essential in an age when motor car ownership was growing. The building of the M1, the country's first long-distance motorway, had already begun in 1959.

There was a predictable outcry over Beeching's recommendations and even the Government, which concurred with much of his thinking, accepted that many of the report's recommendations were too draconian. As a consequence the proposals were considerably modified. Notwithstanding, the national network was still reduced to around 11,000 route miles by the early 1970s, the axe falling mainly upon rural lines, many of which had seen declining traffic for many years. Further reductions followed, albeit at a slower pace, but there was still only limited investment in those lines earmarked for retention until the last two decades of the century, when some lines and stations were reinstated on economic or social grounds.

Twenty years on and following the sale of a number of state-owned utilities and their transfer into the private sector, the railways too were privatized. An Act of Parliament in 1997 passed responsibility for the operation of passenger and freight services to commercial companies, while

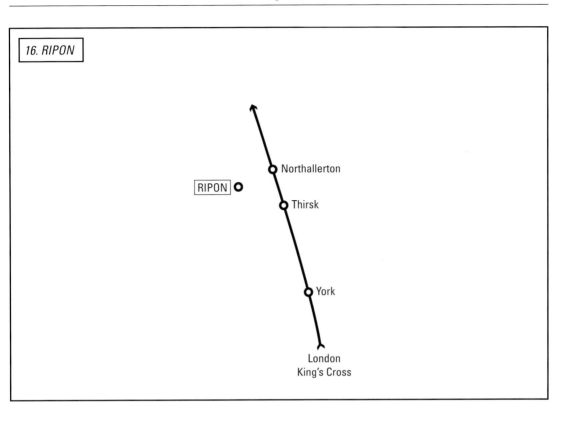

A 225 electric train, the mainstay of services along the East Coast route.

The North Yorkshire Moors Railway, a victim of Dr Beeching's cuts.

the provision of the infrastructure upon which services ran was to remain a national resource. As discussed in Chapter 9, over the fifteen years since privatization, both passenger and freight markets have experienced considerable growth. In parallel, public and private investment has increased although its application to routes has been disproportionate. Nonetheless, the railways are now delivering a better service than at any time in the last fifty years. Demand increases with every year and the debate about how to improve efficiency is conducted with equal intensity.

The railway connecting Leeds to Ripon, opened in 1901 and closed sixty six-years later, was an early casualty of the Beeching review despite its use as a diversionary route when the parallel East Coast main line had to be suspended for operational reasons. There were daily trains from Liverpool to Newcastle and occasional trains to Scotland. At its peak in the inter-war years the line carried considerable traffic. Little now remains of the track bed, some sections having been incorporated into road improvement schemes, making reopening unlikely. However, it must be recognized that since the 1980s a number of Beeching's closure proposals have come to be seen as ill-judged. Some lines have therefore been reinstated with considerable benefit to the communities they originally served. Today there are a number of campaigns across Britain aimed at reopening closed railway arteries, the line serving Ripon being one of them, although its chances of again seeing trains are probably meagre.

Ripon Cathedral

There has been a church here for more than 1,300 years.

Look for Wilfrid's Crypt, the pulpit with its four carved figures of saints, the screen and the 'mechanical hand', which allows the organist to control the choir without leaving the organ loft.

Ripon is a small market town in North Yorkshire. It was here that Wilfrid, who had been educated by the Celtic monks at Lindisfarne and who became one of the earliest missionaries in the North of England, built a Saxon church dating from 672. His was the first church on the site of the present Ripon Cathedral and its Saxon crypt can still be seen beneath the nave altar. A notice adjacent to the crypt entrance states of Wilfrid that 'he believed the crypt to be a copy of the tomb in which the body of Christ was laid and from which he rose on Easter Day.' It has been visited by pilgrims ever since its foundation. Wilfrid travelled widely throughout his life, both within Britain, where he established a number of monasteries, and to Rome. He based some aspects of the design of his cathedral on styles of architecture seen in Italy. That church was destroyed by the Vikings, long after Wilfrid's death in 709.

The present cathedral dates from the late twelfth century when Roger de Pont l'Eveque was the Archbishop of York. There was always a close association in medieval times between Ripon and York Minster. York was the centre of the archdiocese and minsters, or 'missionary centres', were established at Ripon and Beverley in Yorkshire and at Southwell in Nottinghamshire, all churches under the authority of the archbishops of York. Subsequent archbishops like Walter de Grey, who began the building of the present Gothic minster in York, and John Romanus, one of his successors, probably exerted considerable influence over the development of the cathedral in Ripon in their time.

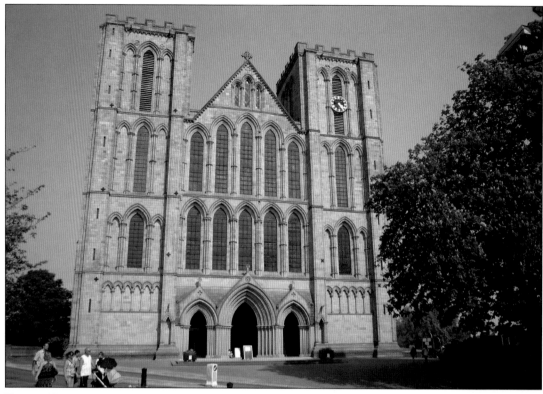

The west front of Ripon Cathedral.

Much of the cathedral was rebuilt in the Perpendicular style in the late fifteenth century following the collapse of the central tower. The nave and its side aisles are wide and spacious and incorporate building work undertaken over a number of years. The wooden roof was designed by Sir George Gilbert Scott in the 1860s and is based upon the medieval design of the York Minster transept roofs. The pulpit, made in 1913, is constructed in marble and copper and is adorned by four bronze figures representing the Anglo-Saxon saints Cuthbert, Chad, Hilda and Etheldreda.

The *pulpitum*, or screen, which separates the nave from the quire, was rebuilt after the central tower collapsed in 1450. It is similar to the screen in York Minster and was adorned with statues of benefactors, although most of these were destroyed in the sixteenth century and later. They were replaced in 1947 by

The east window.

statues of figures relevant to the cathedral's history. The north transept contains the tombs of the Markinfield family of nearby Markinfield Hall, whose burial place it was, while monuments in the south transept commemorate past owners of the Studley Royal estate adjacent to Fountains Abbey. The two transepts contain the most extensive remains of Archbishop Roger's original cathedral.

The quire is arranged in a traditional way with places for the clergy and the College of Canons strictly allocated according to position and importance. Below the organ loft just inside the entrance to the quire is a mechanical hand, installed in 1695, which could be used by the organist to direct the choir without his having to leave his seat at the organ. As in other cathedrals, misericords can be found beneath the seats in the quire stalls, each carved with angels or animals according to the imagination of the carver. The reredos behind the high altar was carved in 1923 in memory of those who died in the First World War. Above it is a large figure of the risen Christ. The East Window dates from the middle of the nineteenth century and celebrates the formation of the Diocese of Ripon in 1836.

The west end of the cathedral has very recently undergone extensive change following the installation of glass doors in 2012. Their creation has been very beneficial in that they allow more light into the nave and permit an uninterrupted view from the nave altar into the streets beyond the cathedral.

The quire screen.

Only a few miles to the west of Ripon and close to the road towards Pateley Bridge stands Fountains Abbey, founded by Cistercian monks seeking a life of austerity. They had apparently become disenchanted with the routine that they had hitherto undergone at St Mary's Abbey in York and in 1132 travelled to Ripon and set up a new abbey on land given to them by the Archbishop of York. Over the centuries the abbey was developed into an important monastic centre until it was plundered by Henry VIII in 1539 at the time of the Reformation. No account of the lives led by Christians in the Ripon area would be complete without reference to Fountains or indeed a visit to the ruins of the abbey.

Successive churches in Ripon have provided a Christian presence in the area for more than 1,300 years. In its time the present cathedral has been a minster, later downgraded to the status of a parish church and more recently in 1836 raised to the position of a cathedral, the mother church of the

The north side of the cathedral.

present diocese. In 2000 the name of the diocese was changed to that of Ripon and Leeds. It remains to be seen whether its fortunes will change again since, as I write, a plan has been mooted that suggests that the Ripon bishopric may be incorporated into a larger Yorkshire diocese. This would see the amalgamation of the dioceses of Ripon and Leeds and Wakefield – and possibly also Bradford – into a single bishopric based upon the cathedral at Wakefield. Meanwhile, with St Wilfrid's Crypt dating from 672, Ripon will always be entitled to claim to be one of the oldest of English cathedrals.

East Anglia

Lincoln Cathedral.

Chapter 17

Lincoln and Peterborough

■ **Lincoln Cathedral** ■ the importance of St Hugh ■ some less frequented railways of East Anglia
■ **Peterborough Cathedral** ■ where two queens were buried
■ the world speed record for a steam locomotive ■

Getting There

Direct train services from London to Lincoln are very few considering the importance of the city and not necessarily convenient to the traveller. However, by taking an East Coast mainline express to the north and changing into a connecting service at Peterborough, Newark or Doncaster, Lincoln can be reached in less than two-and-a-half hours from London.

Peterborough is fifty minutes from King's Cross; Newark about seventy-five minutes and Doncaster around an hour and a half. The onward journey to Lincoln from Newark is less than an hour; from Peterborough and Doncaster it is over an hour.

The journey connecting Lincoln to Peterborough via Sleaford and Spalding takes one hour and twenty minutes.

Railway Notes

Visits to Lincoln and Peterborough were amongst the first undertaken in researching this book and I chose to journey to the two cities by going first to Lincoln via a change at Doncaster, and then to Peterborough. I travelled between the two cathedrals by a route originally managed jointly by the Great Northern and Great Eastern Railway companies prior to the 1923 Act of Parliament that incorporated both into the London & North Eastern Railway. I chose this route because it offers more of interest to the railway enthusiast. There are alternative routes to both cathedrals as set out at the head of this chapter, all of which are equally convenient. It is feasible to visit both cathedrals in one day, although it will be a long one.

Doncaster is a bleak and austere station with little to recommend it other than the multiplicity of services that call there giving connections across the country. Journeying eastwards from the town the train to Lincoln first travels towards the river Trent, Middle England's largest river, which it crosses at Gainsborough, an inland port dominated by an enormous power station. The flat landscape gets flatter and seemingly wetter the closer you get to Lincoln. The cathedral stands high above the surrounding countryside on a limestone ridge, suggestive of a ship stranded upon a rocky foreshore, and can be seen from all directions long before the city is reached. When floodlit at night it presents an even more imposing sight.

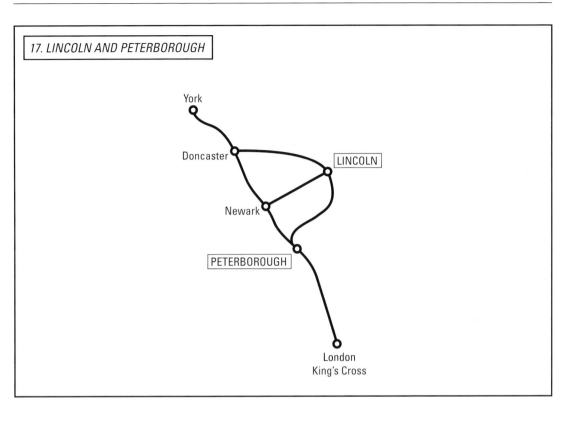

17. LINCOLN AND PETERBOROUGH

York

Doncaster

LINCOLN

Newark

PETERBOROUGH

London
King's Cross

York Station. An example of one of the many impressive railway stations built in Britain in the twentieth century.

Lincoln Cathedral

The splendid Gothic cathedral, built in the twelfth century, dominates the city and surrounding countryside and is one of England's earliest Norman churches.

Look for the west front with its frieze, the spacious area and the pillars of the nave, the Bishop's Eye and the Dean's Eye in the transepts, St Hugh's Quire and the Lincoln Imp on the north side of the Angel Quire.

Apart from the distant prospect of the cathedral there is little to tell a visitor that he is approaching one of Christendom's most glorious churches as his train nears the city. Lincoln itself is not an attractive place. Moreover, reaching the Cathedral Quarter from the station involves a twenty-minute walk up a hill that becomes progressively steeper the higher you climb. However, the climb is well worthwhile since Lincoln Cathedral has much to show the visitor.

Like so many places in Britain early attempts to establish a centre of worship at Lincoln were curtailed by disaster. The first bishop, Remigius, instructed by William the Conqueror to build a cathedral suitable 'to reflect God's power and authority' and to be the centre of a diocese of the same name, completed a Norman cathedral shortly before the close of the eleventh century.

The west front of Lincoln Cathedral.

The high altar.

A fire in 1141 and an earthquake forty years later destroyed most of that church and it was not until the arrival of Bishop Hugh in 1186 that work started on a replacement. It was Hugh who began the building of the present magnificent structure, working from the east end to build in the Gothic style, eventually joining it to what was left of the Norman west front. The latter, with its wonderful frieze of biblical scenes, had been built by his predecessors, Bishops Remigius and Alexander. Even after its completion the cathedral was not without its troubles, the central tower collapsing in 1237, later being rebuilt with a wooden spire that remained in place until blown down in 1548.

Bishop Hugh was a much revered figure and following his death in 1200 was canonized twenty years later. His name constantly crops up during a tour of the cathedral. Originally the diocese of Lincoln covered an area from the Humber to the Thames and was controlled from Dorchester in the Thames Valley. The centre of the diocese was moved to Lincoln on completion of Hugh's cathedral, since when its area of authority has been reduced as the population of East Anglia has grown and more dioceses have been created.

The West Window is of Victorian glass and is dominated by a rose window in memory of Bishop Remigius. Entering the nave the visitor is immediately struck by the spaciousness of the cathedral, its lofty pillars and vaulting, with windows of Victorian stained glass on either side depicting scenes from the two testaments. The baptismal font, adjacent to the south-west end of

The Great East Window.

the nave, dates from the twelfth century. It is made of Belgian marble and is carved with a frieze of mythical wild beasts; these symbolize the battle between good and evil with which a Christian must come to terms before being baptised. Baptism has always been perceived as the start of an individual's journey through Christian life. A font is normally positioned near the principal entrance to a church and invariably, but not always, towards the west end of the building.

Considerable damage was inflicted upon the nave of Lincoln Cathedral during the Civil War when Cromwell's troops were billeted inside the building; windows were damaged and the figures on the Norman west end allegedly used for target practice by ill-disciplined soldiers. For similar reasons there is little or no brass in the building, much of it having been looted. Exceptions are the lectern and chandeliers in the quire.

The transepts are of a similar height to the nave and much of the glass is medieval, being either thirteenth- or fourteenth-century. The south transept is dominated by a circular rose or 'wheel' window called the Bishop's Eye. It looks south to welcome pilgrims journeying to worship at the cathedral on the hill. In the north transept is a corresponding window known as the Dean's Eye, built later, 'to ward off evil from the north'. The quire screen below the central tower is carved with a variety of leering and grinning human heads as well as flowers and many different creatures. In medieval times sermons were often delivered by priests standing on top of the

The Dean's Eye in Lincoln Cathedral faces north.

Opposite, the Bishop's Eye faces south.

183

The east end and chapter house.

screen and addressing those assembled in the nave below. In an aisle leading north out of the main part of the cathedral towards the cloisters is a facsimile of Lincoln's copy of the *Magna Carta*; the original has recently been loaned to various exhibitions in America, a country with which the cathedral has links. *See also* Chapter 5 recording details of Salisbury Cathedral's copy of the *Magna Carta*.

St Hugh's Quire beyond the screen is where most services are sung. It is the heart of the cathedral, where the dean and canons have their stalls and the bishop his *cathedra*. Its designation as St Hugh's Quire further reinforces the age-old debt the cathedral owes him. Further east still is the Angel Quire, so named because of the many angels carved on the stonework; this area of the cathedral was added in 1280 and contains the shrine of St Hugh, to which many miracles have been attributed over the years. A chart explaining the layout of the quire says of St Hugh, 'He spoke God's testimonies before kings and were not ashamed' – a fitting epithet for a great churchman.

The nave looking east.

The Great East Window dominates the eastern end, with its stained glass recounting stories from the Bible, while high up on a north side arch of the Angel Quire is a carving of the Lincoln Imp, a figure whose origins are shrouded in mystery. Was he a real devil who made such a nuisance of himself that the angels turned him to stone? Visitors will need to go to Lincoln to discover, in the process following in the footsteps of the multitude of pilgrims and worshippers who have travelled there for more than nine centuries to visit what must be one of England's most imposing and best celebrated churches.

Railway Notes

From Lincoln I boarded a second train, which took me via Sleaford and Spalding to Peterborough. Apart from touching the edges of the Lincolnshire Wolds south of Sleaford, the line traverses flat, featureless countryside, much of it criss-crossed by water channels. This heralds a close proximity to the fens and indeed these begin only a few miles to the east. Glasshouses and polytunnels for growing vegetables, field upon field of cabbages and the occasional windmill, all overlaid by a lowering grey sky, were the only signs of human endeavour. Not even the passage of the train stirred much interest and we were a small band of travellers who eventually arrived at Peterborough.

For the railway enthusiast this leg of the journey reeks of nostalgia. A profusion of semaphore signals and large wooden telegraph poles with their crosspieces and enamel conductors still intact but with the wires long since removed, followed the train's progress, suggesting that little investment had reached the line in recent years. Jointed track with bullhead rails that gives rise to that familiar, reassuring tattoo that results when a steel wheel encounters a joint between two steel rails, added to the impression that I was travelling in a railway time warp. However, this may not be the case for much longer; the 86-mile 'round about' route from Doncaster to Peterborough is already used as a diversionary railway when the parallel East Coast main line has to be closed for maintenance. There is conjecture in railway circles that the whole route will soon be upgraded to take more traffic, in particular freight, as an alternative to the main line.

The extent to which freight is transported by rail is often underestimated. While road vehicles generally carry a far larger proportion of the nation's goods, rail freight is growing, especially in the bulk transport sector where many lorryloads can be moved in a single train, both more economically and more quickly. I believe that this trend is set to continue as the environmental advantages of rail transport come to be better recognized and the road network becomes ever more saturated. Commodities like coal, steel, oil and motor vehicles have for many years used rail and more recently some of the country's supermarket chains have chosen to move stocks in bulk the same way. Since 1830, mail has been carried by rail in Travelling Post Office trains, which can sort the post and collect and deliver mailbags at lineside gantries without the need to stop. However, transport of mail by rail ceased in 2004 in favour of delivery by air and road, although there have been recent indications that some of this traffic may be returning, if only on a seasonal basis.

How rail traffic in all areas will develop must depend to a great extent upon the results of the Government's deliberations as to whether and where to build a high-speed line to link London to the Midlands, the North and Scotland, similar to the line that already connects St Pancras Station with the Continent through the Channel Tunnel. The debate will no doubt be protracted and often acrimonious but it seems inevitable that such a route will eventually be built if Britain is in future to compete economically with its Continental partners. *See also* Chapters 1 and 14.

Peterborough Cathedral

A fine Norman cathedral, once the burial place of two queens.

Look for the design of the west front, the view east along the nave, Queen Catherine of Aragon's tomb, the site where Mary Queen of Scots was once buried, the New Building and the Hedda Stone.

Peterborough Cathedral is only a ten-minute walk from the railway station. A monastery is believed to have been built on the site as early as 655. Following a Viking raid in 870, a second, Benedictine, abbey was then built, surviving until 1116 when it was destroyed in a fire. The present Norman cathedral was built between 1118 and 1238, although it did not attain cathedral status until 1541 when the abbey was dissolved during the Reformation. It is an impressive building and should be approached from the west to enable a visitor to appreciate the building's fine lines.

The thirteenth-century west front formed with three Gothic porticos is probably unique. The central arch of the front leans slightly outwards although whether this is due to subsidence or was intended in order to create an optical illusion to make the central portico appear more imposing

The west front of Peterborough Cathedral.

The nave.

The shrine of Queen Catherine of Aragon.

is unclear. Like with so many of our cathedrals, theories abound as to why they were built in the way they were, which is what makes exploring them so interesting.

The nave with its beautiful wooden ceiling was completed around 1250, although it has been repainted and, more recently, cleaned. After you enter from the west end you first encounter the font, made from Alwalton marble, dating from the thirteenth century. The nave, impressive for its height and its massive piers and completed in 1197 using local cream-coloured Barnack stone, is dominated by a hanging crucifix just before the central tower with the inscription 'The Cross stands while the world turns'. It was designed in the 1970s. There is no quire screen and so, when standing at the west end, you get a clear view all the way to the apse; the hanging crucifix enhances this view and helps to mitigate any tunnel effect.

The central tower was originally intended to be higher and has had to be rebuilt twice. The first construction proved too heavy and was later reconstructed to include a lighter lantern tower. The tower was rebuilt again in the nineteenth century after it was found that movement had taken place and the structure had weakened, causing it to be declared unsafe. The stones, wooden beams and roof bosses were replaced exactly as they were originally built in the fourteenth century.

Following her death at Kimbolton Castle in 1536, Catherine of Aragon, the first wife of Henry VIII, was buried in a side aisle between the apse and the presbytery at Peterborough. *See also*

The baptismal font in Peterborough Cathedral.

Chapter 8, which refers to Catherine's earlier marriage to Prince Arthur, Henry VIII's elder brother, who is buried at Worcester. Fifty-one years after Queen Catherine's death, Mary Queen of Scots was also buried at Peterborough, on the opposite side of the presbytery, following her execution at nearby Fotheringay in 1587. Her remains were moved to Westminster Abbey in 1612 on the instructions of her son, James I.

The New Building at the east end, beyond the circular apse, was constructed between 1596 and 1609. The fan-vaulting design of the roof is spectacular and was developed later in the construction of King's College Chapel, Cambridge. Lying in the New Building is the Hedda Stone, one of the few surviving remnants of the abbey of Saxon times dating from around 870.

Peterborough Cathedral presents the visitor with a lovely, spacious ambience, an uncomplicated, almost low-key building when compared with some of its grander contemporaries. Partly hidden from view by a modern shopping mall, it could easily be missed. Indeed, until I set out to write this book I had only ever seen its pinnacles and towers from a train passing through Peterborough Station en route from London to the North and had never contemplated a visit. That oversight has now been rectified.

Railway Notes

The East Coast main line will have been travelled countless times by those who may read this book. Going north from Peterborough and after only a few miles a stretch of line is reached where the world speed record for a steam locomotive hauling carriages was achieved in 1938. On 3 July that year, Sir Nigel Gresley's A4 Pacific locomotive *Mallard* recorded a speed of 126mph shortly after emerging from Stoke Tunnel and heading south towards London. It is a record never surpassed. *Mallard* remained in service until the early 1960s and is now preserved at the National Railway Museum in York. The museum, located only a few minutes from the station, houses a wonderful display of locomotives, rolling stock and railway memorabilia from early Victorian times to the present day. Amongst its exhibits are an enormous Chinese steam locomotive, probably the biggest ever built, a carriage of the Japanese 'bullet train' and two of Britain's own celebrated steam locomotives, *Flying Scotsman* and *Coronation Scot*. A visit to the NRM, which is also touched upon in Chapter 13, will tell you more about Britain's railway history and how she led the world in developing 'the iron road', than any number of learned tomes or technical journals.

Mallard.

Chapter 18

Southwell

■ A town without a railway connection ■ **Southwell Minster** ■ close links with York Minster ■

Getting There

Southwell (pronounced 'Suthell') is not on a railway route, although the Newark to Nottingham local line passes within a few miles to the south of the town and the nearest station at Fiskerton could be used. From London the easiest way to reach Southwell is to travel from King's Cross by the East Coast main line to Newark, a journey of around seventy-five minutes, and to then take a taxi or bus to Southwell, less than 10 miles to the west.

There are also good rail connections to Newark from York, Lincoln and Peterborough, so a visit to Southwell Minster can, if wished, be combined with a visit to any of those three cathedrals.

Southwell Minster

One of only two Anglican cathedrals still styled a minster and whose Christian origins go back more than a thousand years.

Look for the barrel-vaulted ceiling, the bread pews in the south transept, the Eagle Lectern in the quire and the triptych in the Airmen's Chapel, and visit the chapter house.

Southwell is a small town in the valley of the river Trent. It has never been directly served by the railway and, when visiting, the traveller must rely upon road connections to complete his journey from the nearby main line station at Newark. The undisturbed, rather sleepy aura of the place may be explained by this absence of sophisticated communications; Southwell is a pleasant market town.

Originally a southern outpost of the Diocese of York, the church, established in the twelfth century, only achieved cathedral status in 1884 when the diocese of Southwell was created to meet a requirement to cater for growing populations. Today the bishop presides over an area that encompasses most of Nottinghamshire and some parts of the neighbouring county of Derbyshire. More recently the title of the diocese was changed to more accurately reflect its geographic responsibilities and was re-designated the Diocese of Southwell and Nottingham.

The connection between Southwell and York goes back many centuries. In 956, Oskytel, the Archbishop of York, was granted land, upon which a small Saxon church was built. This church, similar to some other churches in the York diocese, was termed a minster because it was probably the largest church in the area and a base from where its priests would go out to teach the Christian faith to people in the surrounding villages. This would in all probability have been before parishes

191

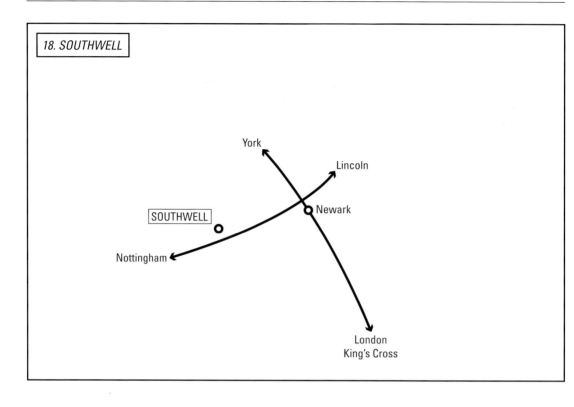

18. SOUTHWELL

York

Lincoln

SOUTHWELL   Newark

Nottingham

London
King's Cross

Southwell Cathedral's 'pepper pot' western towers.

The Band of the Coldstream Guards rehearsing for a concert in the nave.

came to be established. In medieval times Southwell Minster was in effect a satellite of York, just as Beverley and Ripon were in other parts of the archbishop's jurisdiction. Interestingly, the term 'minster model' is increasingly used in the Anglican Church to describe a situation where, in order to use limited numbers of clergy to best effect, priests may be based upon a principal central church. From there they can be deployed to meet the needs of parishes within the local area that may not have their own resident clergyman.

The rebuilding of the original Saxon church in 1108 was authorized by Archbishop Thomas of York, who already had a manor house in Southwell, and construction of the nave and tower, containing some of the oldest parts of the minster, began thereafter. Oskytel's original Saxon church is thought to have been demolished around 1130 and the main part of the new minster completed towards the end of the century, although several refinements were made later. For instance, the spires of the twin western towers, known locally as 'the pepper pots' and completed in 1170, were judged to be unsafe at the beginning of the nineteenth century and were demolished. They were restored in the 1880s.

Moving up the nave from the west end the visitor will immediately be struck by the solid nature of the building. The columns, which rise through three levels to form the main part of the nave, are of classic Romanesque style and give an impression of great permanence. The roof, originally horizontal, was destroyed in 1711 when fire broke out in one of the towers and was later

The nave.

The pulpit.

The lectern recovered from a lake in Sherwood Forest.

replaced by a wooden barrel-vaulted ceiling, a construction that I had not encountered since my visit to Carlisle. At the east end of the nave before the crossing and high up is a sculpture of Christ the King, created in 1987 by Peter Ball; as the minster's excellent and very informative *Cathedral Companion* states, this is a figure 'of the risen Christ with arms outstretched, welcoming you to this ancient church and offering comfort, help and sanctuary'.

The Great West Window is modern and was installed in 1996. It was designed and painted by Patrick Reyntiens and, again quoting the *Cathedral Companion*, is described by its creator as 'a gathering of angels, enjoying being with God; just all joy and worship'. On the south side of the nave can be seen the font, a replacement for the original, which was destroyed at the time of Cromwell's Republic and which has a suspended wooden cover. Further east along the nave is the pulpit, which dates from 1896. It was carved by G.F. Bodley and its six figures all have close connections with York, thereby again reinforcing the ancient links between there and Southwell. Shown are St Paulinus, the first bishop of the northern province of Britain who in 627 baptized King Edwin of Northumbria in a wooden church in York. It is believed that church was the first York Minster. Also displayed are figures of Queen Ethelburga of Kent, whom Edwin married and who had herself been converted to Christianity by St Augustine, the first Archbishop of Canterbury, and Mary the Mother of Jesus shown holding the Infant Christ. *See also* Chapter 13.

The two transepts contain several items of interest. On the south side are two 'bread pews', which date from the fifteenth century and were so named because they were set aside for the destitute to occupy in order that they might be given money and food. Underneath one end of the front pew is an area of mosaic tiling that may have been part of the floor of the Saxon church and could have come from an earlier Roman villa, originally close to the site of the minster. On the north side is the fine tomb of Edwyn Sandys, an archbishop of York who died in 1588, one of six archbishops who occupied the palace at Southwell but the only one to have a tomb in the minster. Also in the transept is a carved lintel stone, or tympanum, which is thought to have originated between the ninth and eleventh centuries. It is unclear whether it originated in the Saxon church or was brought from elsewhere.

Moving from the crossing to enter the quire the visitor must pass through the narrow entrance of the *pulpitum*, or quire screen, apparently so built as to restrict access to the bishop, his clergy and the choir. Started around 1340, after which construction of the main part of the minster is generally assumed to have been finished and since when little of the fabric has been materially altered, the screen is beautifully carved. Above it is the organ, positioned so that its music can fill both the quire and the nave.

Just beyond the entrance to the quire is the Eagle Lectern, which was given to the minster by a dean of Lincoln. Dating from 1503, it was originally in the possession of the monks at Newstead Abbey in nearby Sherwood Forest; when threatened by the ravages of the Reformation in the reign of Henry VIII the monks apparently tied the lectern to a rope and lowered it into a nearby lake to avoid it being removed by the monarch. There it remained for 200 years until eventually hauled to the surface and given to Southwell Minster.

The architectural style of the quire is Early English as opposed to the Romanesque of the nave and tower. Changes were made to the quire during the thirteenth century because it had become too small for its original purpose. This work was authorized by Archbishop Walter de Grey in 1234, who in 1220 had also initiated the early stages of the construction of the fourth and present-day York Minster.

The bishop's quire stall on the south side adjacent to the aisle is known as Wolsey's Stall; it was here that Cardinal Wolsey, Archbishop of York until 1530, spent much of the last year of his life. However, the bishop's *cathedra* is situated on the north side of the chancel just below the Great East Window. The window consists of eight lancets. The top four were made in 1876 and show the Four Evangelists while those below record scenes from the life of Christ. The latter were painted by Jean Chastellain in 1528 and were originally in a church in Paris; when the church was sold during the French Revolution the windows ended up in a shop, where they were discovered by a local Nottinghamshire benefactor who subsequently brought them to Southwell.

Off the north quire aisle is the Airmen's Chapel, which commemorates Air Force personnel killed in war and also contains a memorial to those Polish prisoners of war murdered in Katyn Forest in 1941. The triptych is by Hamish Moyle and takes Dame Edith Sitwell's poem *Still Falls the Rain* as its message. The outer picture shows the death of peace while that inside depicts the resurrection of peace after the rain, linked by the last line of the poem: *Still do I love, still shed my innocent light, my Blood, for thee.* The complete poem is recorded on an explanatory board.

Perhaps Southwell's most wonderful treasure is its chapter house. Built as an octagon towards the close of the thirteenth century it has no central column and the weight of the stone vaulting is carried by a series of flying buttresses. It is one of the few such buildings constructed in this way in Britain. The carvings both inside the chapter house and at the entrance are well worth study although some were damaged at the time of the Civil War. Carvings include foliage, animals and, above the seats of the canons who met daily in the chapter house in medieval times, 'green men' faces, those fantasy figures of ancient lore.

Southwell is probably the smallest town in Britain to be host to a cathedral whose diocesan bishop has responsibility for the care of so many souls. It is also one of only two English cathedrals to be still styled a minster, the other being York. I found my day in its precincts a delight both for the intriguing discoveries that I made and also for the simple and informed manner in which the church was explained both in literature and by those on duty.

The north side of Southwell Cathedral.

Chapter 19

Ely, Norwich and St Edmundsbury

■ The case for further electrification ■ **Ely Cathedral** ■ a symbol of Norman power
■ **Norwich Cathedral** ■ 900 years of history ■ **St Edmundsbury Cathedral**
■ a wartime act of great courage

Getting There

These three cathedrals can be visited in any order from London.

Ely is reached from King's Cross by a modern electric train taking approximately one-and-a-half hours. Norwich from Liverpool Street Station takes less than two hours, again by an electrified service.

There are no direct trains from London to Bury St Edmunds, the location of St Edmundsbury Cathedral. However, by transferring at Stowmarket from a Liverpool Street to Norwich service into a local train, Bury St Edmunds can be reached in less than two hours from the capital.

Local services connect Ely to Norwich and Norwich to Bury St Edmunds via Stowmarket. All journeys take less than two hours.

Railway Notes

Many rail routes in East Anglia were closed following the Beeching Review of the 1960s. The remaining passenger services are generally fast and convenient and provide excellent connections within the region. The line between Peterborough and Ely is especially important since it connects two major electrified rail arteries from London to the North. Were the 20 miles of track between the two towns to be electrified, trains would be able to reach Peterborough or Ely by two parallel routes from London, giving considerable flexibility should either route need to be closed for operational reasons. As recent winters have shown, high winds and heavy snow can quickly disrupt railway operations by bringing down overhead electric cables, thereby immobilizing a train. Such occurrences can result in hours of delay as alternative routes are arranged and replacement diesel traction activated, generating considerable frustration for the travelling public. The cost of the electrification of a few miles of track need not be exorbitant and would permit greater operational flexibility.

Another route that must be a candidate for eventual electrification is the line that links the port of Felixstowe to Peterborough by way of Ipswich and Ely. Sections of this line are already 'wired' and completion of an electrified through route would enable the growing commercial traffic entering the country through Felixstowe to be sent across East Anglia to reach the Midlands, the North of England and Scotland, rather than as happens today when much of it has to be sent by a longer route through the outer suburbs of North London. For many years rail industry leaders have advocated further railway electrification. The clear benefits of greater efficiency and cleaner energy have to be balanced against the capital costs and the achievement of other national priorities. However, a welcome programme of investment in further national electrification was announced in 2010, some of which is already being implemented.

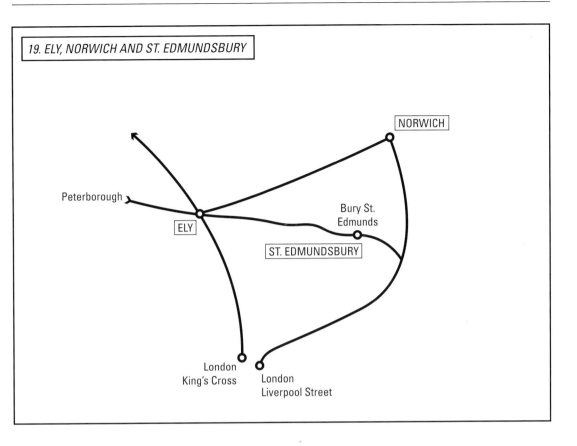

19. ELY, NORWICH AND ST. EDMUNDSBURY

NORWICH

Peterborough

ELY

Bury St.
Edmunds

ST. EDMUNDSBURY

London
King's Cross

London
Liverpool Street

Ely Cathedral

Described as the 'Ship of the Fens' much of the bishop's diocese can be seen from the cathedral's twelfth-century west tower.

Look out for the labyrinth at the west end, the painted nave ceiling, the octagon and the attached Lady chapel.

In this chapter I propose to visit the three East Anglian cathedrals by a circular route from London encompassing Ely, Norwich and Bury St Edmunds. It is feasible to do this over two days with an overnight stop in Norwich.

Approaching Ely from any direction travellers will get their first sight of the cathedral many miles before they arrive in the city. Ely Cathedral is rightly described as the 'Ship of the Fens', dominating the land around it for a considerable distance. There has been a church on the site since 673 when Etheldreda, a Saxon princess, founded a monastery in Ely for men and women, although they were strictly segregated. That church was destroyed by the Vikings in 870 but was restored a hundred years later as a Bendictine abbey.

Ely takes its name from 'eel island', a waterlogged area of the Fens where the snake-like fish were plentiful in watercourses in medieval times. After the Norman invasion of 1066, Hereward the Wake defended the abbey and surrounding settlement from William the Conqueror's armies but was eventually driven from the island in 1071. William then appointed Simeon to be the Abbot of Ely and in 1081 he began the building of the present-day cathedral, which was completed in 1189.

Like most cathedrals Ely is built in the form of a cross. The oldest parts of the Norman building are the west end, the nave and the transepts. The nave at a length of 248 feet is one of the longest in England while the west tower rises to a height of 215 feet, from where much of the diocese of which the cathedral is the centre can be seen. Originally the tower was flanked by two transepts but that on the north-western side was demolished when the tower was heightened. The surviving south-west transept was restored in 1844 and has one of the best-preserved Romanesque interiors in England. By the Galilee Porch and just inside the west door, and marked out on the floor, is a labyrinth that, if followed, will take a walker a distance equating to the height of the tower above; walking a labyrinth was an ancient spiritual discipline believed to carry an individual through life's trials and tribulations to meet their God.

The nave ceiling was restored in Victorian times and tells the story of Christ's ancestry from Adam to the Virgin Mary. There are twelve panels, the first six painted by Henry Styleman-Lestrange and, following his death, the remaining six being completed by Thomas Gambier-Parry. To the untutored eye it may be difficult to detect a change of artistic style between panels six and seven. The Prior's Door, which used to give access to the cloisters, can be found to one side of the south nave aisle. It dates from 1135 and above the door Christ is shown, enthroned in Heaven, while around the sides of the door are many carvings of birds and animals.

Ely Cathedral.

The nave, showing the painted ceiling.

Moving further east to the crossing the visitor comes to the Octagon Tower. The original Norman tower collapsed in February 1322 just after the first service of the day had ended with, fortunately, no one being hurt. The explanation for the collapse is said to have been the work being carried out to build the nearby Lady chapel, where the foundations were being dug at the time. Removal of soil may have caused changes to the water table, leading to the ground beneath the tower drying out and becoming unstable.

Following the collapse it was decided to build an octagonal lantern tower. The Octagon was first built on the floor of the crossing, then dismantled and hauled into position and reassembled 140 feet above ground. The work was supervised by one of the monks, Alan of Walsingham, and built by William Hurley, Edward III's master carpenter.

The Octagon is 71 feet in width and the boss depicting Christ at its centre is 142 feet above the ground. The combined weight of the wood and lead used in its construction is 400 tons and it took twenty years to build. The panels around the base of the lantern are decorated with thirty-two painted angels representing a heavenly host singing Psalm 150: *O Praise God in his holiness: praise him in the firmament of his power.* The roof of the tower is fan-vaulted. Many of the timbers holding the Octagon in position are original although some strengthening has been necessary. The tower must be Ely's finest treasure both in its magnificence and as a wonder of medieval engineering.

It is possible to join a guided tour that takes the visitor up a number of narrow stairways within the octagon tower and onto the roof of the cathedral, although such an excursion is not recommended for anybody without a head for heights.

The Octagon Tower and Lady chapel.

The western tower and south-west transept.

The north transept contains a wall painting depicting St Edmund, King of East Anglia, who in the ninth century resisted the Viking invasion of the province. He was killed for refusing to deny his faith, being tied to a tree and 'shot through' with arrows. It is high up on the north wall of the transept. St Edmund was buried at Bury St Edmunds, the site of the third cathedral I visited in East Anglia.

The quire was rebuilt in the fourteenth century and contains intricately carved stalls and misericords. This part of the cathedral and the side aisles suffered considerable change at the time of the Reformation in 1539. Extremist supporters of Henry VIII destroyed many memorials and images so that, as the cathedral guide book puts it, 'no remains or memory of them might be found in the future.' Beyond the quire is the presbytery, built in the thirteenth century to accommodate St Etheldreda's shrine; the tomb was destroyed during the Reformation and the site is now only marked by a black marble slab set into the floor.

The Lady chapel on the north-east side of the cathedral and adjacent to the quire was completed in

Angels painted inside the Octagon Tower.

View of the quire from the Octagon Tower.

1349 and is dedicated to the Virgin Mary. It is the largest chapel of its kind in any English cathedral. Its original stained glass windows and painted walls were destroyed during the Reformation. Today the clear glass in its windows and its unadorned walls make it a bright if rather empty place. A new statue of the Virgin Mary by David Wynne was installed in 2000 and shows the Virgin proclaiming the soon to be born Messiah.

A tombstone in the south porch of the cathedral will delight the railway enthusiast. It commemorates two local men, both of whom died on Christmas Eve 1845, and takes the form of some verse entitled *The Spiritual Railway*. It begins with the words: *The Line to Heaven by Christ was made, with heavenly truth the Rails were laid*. The complete lyric is reproduced in the frontispiece to this book.

Cathedrals built in Norman times were not only created as memorials to God but were also intended as symbols of political power. They and the grand castles of the same period were built to impress and intimidate local populations into understanding and accepting that the Norman invaders were here to stay. Cathedrals like Ely and Norwich are perfect examples of how Norman power was projected to overawe the vanquished.

After Ely the railway to Norwich soon leaves the featureless Fen country, running east and following the boundary between the counties of Norfolk and Suffolk to reach Thetford. When the Vikings arrived in East Anglia in the ninth century they made Thetford their capital and the town later became the seat of the bishops of East Anglia, until the latter were transferred to Norwich in 1094.

Norwich Cathedral

A dignified cathedral in an enchanting city; both have experienced considerable turbulence in their long history.

Look for the nave roof, the bosses studding the roofs throughout the cathedral, the misericords in the quire and the apse, where the bishop's *cathedra* can be found.

When built in the eleventh century Norwich Cathedral must have dominated the surrounding countryside in the same way as Ely dominated Fenland. Indeed the spire at Norwich rises to a height of 315 feet, only 14 feet lower than the highest land in the county of Norfolk. Over the intervening years the city has grown considerably in size and modern buildings have tended to dwarf the cathedral, in the process diminishing the initial impact this fine building has on the visitor.

In 1096 Bishop Herbert de Losinga started to build the eastern end of the cathedral and, such was the pace at which work progressed, the building was consecrated in late 1101. By 1145 the cathedral, built in beautiful Caen stone shipped from Normandy, was complete and a Benedictine monastery established. The power of the Church in medieval times was very considerable and the bishop and the prior of the monastery soon created a strong religious base that grew in wealth as land and property were accumulated. At the same time the city was growing in importance as trade developed and clashes between church and civic authority soon became unavoidable.

In the first centuries of its existence Norwich Cathedral saw turbulent times. In August 1272 conflict arose between the prior and the people of Norwich over the right to charge fees for fairs

Norwich Cathedral from the south.

on unused ground called Tombland, adjacent to the monastery. Rioting erupted, buildings were destroyed and the interior of the cathedral ransacked. Henry III had to travel to the city to calm the situation and retribution for those responsible was swift and brutal. It took six years to restore the damage and Edward I attended the re-consecration of the cathedral in 1278.

In the middle of the fourteenth century the Black Death, a form of bubonic plague, ravaged Europe and came to Britain in 1348, killing an estimated eighth of the population. A third of the people of Norwich are said to have died. Thirty years later there occurred the Peasant's Revolt, an insurrection against taxation at a time of growing demand for social change. In Norfolk the Bishop of Norwich, Henry Despenser, led an army to quell the local uprising, which he did, seemingly, with little mercy. As if such external events did not present sufficient challenge to the cathedral authorities, 1463 saw the collapse of the cathedral's wooden spire and the destruction of the nave roof and organ. To restore the cathedral to its former state Bishop Walter Lyhart set about reconstructing the nave roof with a vaulted ceiling decorated with bosses. Bosses are not unlike 'knuckles' and are positioned at the junctions where the roof ribs meet; there are more than 1,100 bosses in Norwich Cathedral and each is painted to depict a biblical scene. It should perhaps be remembered that, in medieval times when the majority of the population could neither read nor write, images portrayed on bosses or painted in windows were a means of educating people. The cathedral guide speculates that 'the imagery on bosses appears to have been taken from fifteen religious plays – a popular form of street entertainment – and that possibly the craftsmen responsible for carving the bosses also had responsibility for arranging the street plays.'

Bishop Lyhart also built the Great West Window. The present glass dates from 1854 and the colours are very striking, so much so that when first unveiled they were covered up since they were thought to be too vivid. The window depicts scenes from the life of Christ and Moses.

Lyhart was followed as bishop by James Goldwell, who continued the former's work, extending the vaulted ceiling into the presbytery and rebuilding the spire in 1480. Amongst Anglican cathedrals Norwich's spire is second only to that of Salisbury in height.

The sixteenth and seventeenth centuries again brought disruption to Norwich Cathedral as they did to most other churches in Britain. In 1538 the Benedictine monastery was dissolved after 442 years ruling the cathedral. Because dissolution was not resisted by the monks a monastic institution was recreated almost immediately, but in a secular form. A hundred years later, further turmoil overtook the cathedral and the city when civil war broke out between Charles I's Royalists and the parliamentary forces of Oliver Cromwell.

Zealots invaded the cathedral imposing their puritanical rule and destroying many of its shrines and other imagery. There was even a suggestion that the building itself should be demolished and the stone used to build docks and housing for the poor at neighbouring Great Yarmouth. It was not until the nineteenth century that a serious programme of restoration was started by the Victorians, resulting in the cathedral regaining much of its former glory. The year 1996 saw the celebration of 900 years of its existence since Bishop de Losinga had laid the foundation stone.

There are many features of the cathedral that will draw a visitor's attention. The copper bowl of the font near the west end of the nave came from the former Rowntree Mackintosh confectionery factory in the city and was once used for chocolate making. Also on a pillar on the north side of the nave aisle is a memorial to Osbert Parsley, a chorister who sang in the cathedral for fifty years from 1535. This would have involved him in services throughout the disruption of the Reformation period. His career culminated in his composing a special setting of the *Magnificat* for the visit of Elizabeth I in 1578.

Unlike in other cathedrals the crossing, where the transepts and the main body of the cathedral intersect under the tower, is east of the quire, leading into the presbytery. Bishop Goldwell's work in continuing the vaulted roof into the presbytery can be clearly viewed, as can the magnificence of the quire stalls with their intricately carved misericords.

The apse and east end of Norwich Cathedral.

The baptismal font, originally a receptacle used for chocolate making.

The Great West Window.

Plaque commemorating songman Osbert Parsley.

OSBERT PARSLEY
Osbert Parsley was a "singing man" for fifty years, under four Monarchs, Henry VIII, Edward VI, Mary and Elizabeth I. He served continuously through the dissolution of the monasteries, the Reformation, the re-establishment of the Roman Catholic church under Mary, and the renewal of the Church of England under Elizabeth, and died in 1585.

The east end of the cathedral is built in the form of a semi-circular apse, above which are windows at different heights. This part of the cathedral reflects the various stages of building undertaken, first by the Normans, then at clerestory level in the early fourteenth century, and later by the addition of Bishop Goldwell's vaulted roof of 1480. The bishop's chair, or *cathedra*, is positioned in the centre of the apse looking down to the high altar; while not unique since the bishop's *cathedra* in Chelmsford Cathedral is also placed at the east end, *cathedras* are more usually to be found in the quire or nave of a cathedral.

An ambulatory or walkway passes round the eastern end of the presbytery and is sometimes used for processions during a service. Four chapels can be reached from the ambulatory. In St Luke's Chapel can be seen a reredos painted on wooden boards depicting the Passion, which dates from Bishop Despenser's time. It was hidden at the time of the Civil War to prevent its destruction and was only rediscovered in 1847, it having been used as a work bench for much of the intervening time.

Norwich Cathedral is a beautiful building with much to absorb. Its roof bosses, the vaulted ceiling that runs its entire length and the agreeable lines of the apse all underline the dedicated work of generations of bishops, benefactors and highly skilled craftsmen. East Anglia, a region of Britain well known for its distinctiveness, is rightly proud of its cathedral and how it has survived and been developed over so many centuries.

Norwich is a terminus station for a number of routes linking Norfolk's main centres to the county town. Bury St Edmunds in Suffolk is less than 40 miles to the south and easily reached by train by way of a change at Stowmarket.

St Edmundsbury Cathedral

Both cathedral and town are associated with the Saxon King Edmund, whose remains were brought to the local monastery around 900, following his death at the hands of Viking invaders.

Look for the *Magna Carta* barons' heraldic shields in the quire, the detached tower, the Susanna Window and how the medieval nave, the quire built in the twentieth century and the Millennium Tower have all fitted together.

It was not until just before the First World War that a diocese centred upon Bury St Edmunds was created with boundaries approximately co-terminus with those of the county of Suffolk. St James's Church was selected to be the cathedral or mother church of the Diocese of St Edmundsbury and Ipswich.

View of St Edmundsbury Cathedral showing the contrast between the original nave and the tower and quire built towards the end of the twentieth century.

However, Bury St Edmund's involvement with the Church goes back at least a thousand years before then. In 869, St Edmund, the Saxon king of East Anglia, was killed in battle by the Vikings and his remains were taken to the town and placed in a shrine. Later, and despite long periods of upheaval, a Benedictine monastery was established in Bury, which was accorded the status of an abbey by King Cnut in 1020. Over the ensuing years St Edmund's Abbey developed into a major religious community and a great centre of learning.

In 1214, the barons opposed to King John are said to have met in the abbey church, where they swore on the altar to hold him to the legal stipulations of the *Magna Carta*, signed the following year at Runnymede. The heraldic shields of some of those involved are displayed high up in the quire of the present-day cathedral. Bury St Edmund's ancient civic motto, 'Shrine of a King, Cradle of the Law', reflects the historical significance of both St Edmund and the Runnymede treaty.

St James's Church was built within the abbey precincts. In 1539 the latter was dissolved on the orders of Henry VIII but St James's survived and was in time extended. An artist's impression painted in 1747 and now in the cathedral shows that the western end was the oldest part of that church – a long, low building comprising a nave with a shallow chancel to its east. A detached Norman tower, a few yards to the south, was originally the principal entrance to the abbey and was where the bells of St James's may have been housed and where the present bells are today located.

The quire of St Edmundsbury Cathedral.

Today the cathedral is very different. The nave is still the original although with considerable alterations to its roof, which reached such a state of disrepair in 1861 that the church was declared to be unsafe. After some dissension as to whether the low-pitched existing roof should be retained or replaced with a higher version, it was eventually agreed to make a change. The present roof was built by Sir George Gilbert Scott, amongst whose other well-known designs are St Pancras Station and the Albert Memorial in Hyde Park. He then turned his attention to enlarging the chancel.

Since 1960 the cathedral has undergone further development on a considerable scale. Stephen Sykes Bower, the cathedral architect, first built a new entrance porch, after which he rebuilt and enlarged the chancel, now designated as the quire. His plans were completed when two small transepts and the tower were added, the

The Susannah Window.

latter a millennium project, finished in 2005. As a result St Edmundsbury Cathedral is now an appropriate building to be the principal church of the diocese.

Much of the glass is Victorian and, amongst the windows at the west end, there are depictions of the Creation and the Last Judgement. In the south-west corner is a window containing sixteenth-century glass, the lower half of which tells the Old Testament story of Susanna, a harlot who was tricked and then falsely accused of adultery by the Elders. She was tried, defended by the prophet Daniel and found not guilty, whereupon her accusers were themselves put to death.

Throughout the cathedral are kneelers embroidered by people from Suffolk in the 1960s, each of which bears the name of a parish in the diocese.

On the north-east side of the quire is St Edmund's Chapel, a fitting reminder that it was this ninth-century king and later saint whose remains were brought to Bury St Edmunds for burial, thereby leading to the building of a great medieval abbey. Thereafter there followed the establishment of a town, which rose to be an important regional and commercial centre and, in more recent times, the creation of a cathedral to be the seat of the bishop responsible for the county of Suffolk.

Railway Notes

A train from Bury St Edmunds to Ely takes an hour and completes the circular journey to the three East Anglian cathedrals I undertook when compiling this chapter. Suffolk is a pleasant county with rolling hills and wide vistas, intensively farmed and home to the horse racing industry whose courses and gallops can be seen when passing close to Newmarket. About 10 miles prior to Ely the line passes through Soham, a small agricultural town on the edge of the Fens. It was there on 1 June 1944 that one of the most heroic railway events of the Second World War took place. That night Driver Gimbert and Fireman Nighthall had charge of a freight train carrying munitions and military stores to Ipswich destined for US Air Force units stationed in Eastern England in preparation for the invasion of Europe. Approaching Soham, Gimbert observed that the leading freight wagon of his train was on fire. The fire appeared to be spreading very quickly and, knowing the highly dangerous nature of the freight being transported, he decided to stop, detach the offending wagon and then pull it clear of the other fifty wagons, all of which were loaded with bombs and explosives.

Gimbert stopped his train and Nighthall uncoupled the burning wagon, after which they pulled it clear of the train, intending to draw it past Soham Station to a place where it could be dealt with more safely. As the engine and wagon passed through the station and while Gimbert was briefing the local signalman to stop all other traffic, the wagon exploded, blowing an enormous crater 65 feet wide and 16 feet deep. Nighthall and the signalman were both killed instantly but miraculously Gimbert survived, although seriously injured. The station buildings and several houses in the vicinity were destroyed.

The cause of the fire was never positively identified but it is probable that a spark from the locomotive had ignited some residual sulphur powder, still remaining in the leading wagon from a previous journey. Both Gimbert and Nighthall were awarded the George Cross for their courageous actions that night, which undoubtedly saved Soham from an even greater disaster. Sadly for Nighthall it was to be a posthumous award.

Railways have always had their share of misfortunes, some caused by human error as that recorded in Chapter 14 on the Pennine route to Carlisle, some resulting from natural disasters like the collapse of the Firth of Tay railway bridge in December 1879, while enemy action inflicted enormous damage on the network during the Second World War. Notwithstanding, railways have always provided a very safe mode of transport and developing technology, a highly disciplined attitude to operations by railway staffs and an intense pride in the service provided to the travelling public will ensure that such a record continues.

Chapter 20

St Albans and Chelmsford

■ Cross-London rail links ■ **St Albans Cathedral** ■ **Chelmsford Cathedral** ■ timetables ■

Getting There

St Albans is twenty minutes north of London and can be reached from the low-level station beneath St Pancras International Station. Trains are frequent.

Trains to Chelmsford start from Liverpool Street Station. The journey takes approximately forty minutes depending upon the service selected. Some main line trains to Norwich call at Chelmsford and these give a marginally faster journey time than a local service.

Railway Notes

The logic of including visits to the cathedrals at St Albans and Chelmsford in the same chapter may seem strange since they cannot be reached using a single route from the capital. However, both cities were originally founded in Roman times, are situated just to the north or north-east of London and within an hour of that city. It is quite feasible to visit both places in one day, even if it involves visitors having to retrace their steps.

A London Underground train driver.

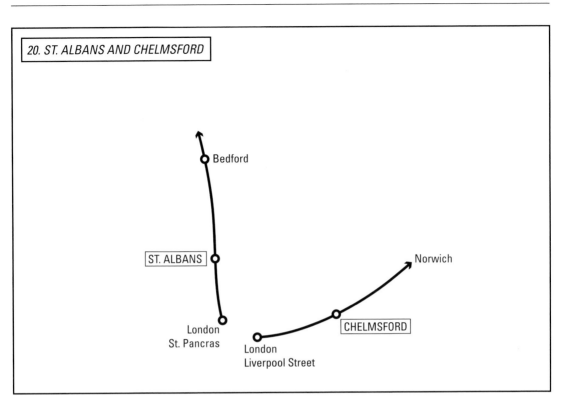

20. ST. ALBANS AND CHELMSFORD

Bedford

ST. ALBANS

Norwich

London
St. Pancras

CHELMSFORD

London
Liverpool Street

London Underground's modern rolling stock.

A suburban train used regularly on electrified routes from Liverpool Street Station.

The suburban line from London to St Albans provides a high-frequency electric service that currently connects St Pancras International Station to places as far north as Bedford. Additionally a large number of services starting from towns south of London now provide a direct route northwards across the city without necessitating a change of train. This south to north service is marketed as Thameslink and, for example, enables passengers to travel seamlessly from Brighton or Gatwick Airport to destinations north of the capital, a welcome development.

The subsurface lines that permit this cross-London transit were originally part of the Metropolitan Railway, built in the 1860s and one of the world's first underground railway networks. Various developments took place over the next century with many of the lines and tunnels eventually becoming redundant as the capital's transport needs altered, until in the 1980s plans to create north to south direct links were formulated. The planning processes were protracted and it was not until 1988 that the first trains ran. Since then further developments have taken place with the building of the new international station at St Pancras and the provision of dual-voltage rolling stock capable of collecting electrical current from overhead wires or a third rail. As a result the electrified systems north and south of the river Thames are now effectively connected. Plans to expand this network are being developed.

Within the next decade a second link will be built across London to connect stations to the west and east of the city, thereby complementing the south to north Thameslink route. This second link is to be known as Crossrail and will connect Maidenhead in the Thames Valley with Shenfield in Essex. The route will comprise 118 kilometres of track and the central section under London will be in tunnels. The political and financial negotiations required to substantiate this second link have been long drawn out and have involved several stakeholders, some with divergent views as to the destinations to be served. It now appears that Heathrow Airport and the Canary Wharf business district could both be linked to the main route, while additional connections could give access to other main lines extending from the capital as well as the high-speed route to the Channel Tunnel.

The decision to serve Heathrow by Crossrail illustrates how difficult transport planning in a metropolis the size of London has become. Now at near capacity the airport is plainly incapable of accepting further growth without very considerable disruption to surrounding communities. The search to find an alternative location east of the capital in Essex, or sited in the Thames Estuary, has now started. A decision to locate in either place could mean current rail expansion plans becoming outmoded soon after their inception. Meanwhile it is hoped that the opening of Crossrail will be achieved in 2017.

St Albans Cathedral

A city and cathedral associated with Britain's first Christian martyr.

Look for the contrasting style of the arches in the nave, the painted insignia on the roof of the quire and tower and the headstone commemorating Archbishop Runcie on the north side of the cathedral.

St Albans, or *Verulamium* as it was called by the Romans, was a garrison town during the Roman occupation of Britain. It was there in 250 that Alban, a Roman who had been converted to Christianity by a local priest, was executed by the authorities. His crime was to shelter and then help the priest to escape. At his trial he refused to acknowledge the pagan Roman gods, instead maintaining that the only true god was Christian, as a result of which he paid the ultimate price for his beliefs.

In the eighth century the Saxons built a monastery near the site of Alban's place of execution and in 793 King Offa of Mercia successfully requested the Pope to allow Alban to be canonized, whereupon the settlement surrounding the monastery came to be called St Albans. Alban was the first Christian martyr and his story is celebrated in the town each year towards the end of June.

The original St Albans Cathedral was a Norman church started in 1077 by Paul de Caen. He demolished much of the existing Saxon monastery, replacing it with a new building using many of the bricks originally made by the Romans, some of which had been lying unused since the destruction of *Verulamium* more than 600 years earlier. When finished in 1115 the abbey church was the largest in England. As the cathedral guidebook says, 'the Roman bricks were too hard to be carved so the round top arches were plastered and painted in a style unique in this country.' In its heyday St Albans Abbey was a thriving Benedictine monastery with a large number of monks led by a succession of highly respected abbots. Although never admitted to the Abbey, Nicholas Breakespear, the only Englishman ever to become Pope, was educated at the adjoining school. He was allegedly thought to be insufficiently intelligent to be admitted to the monastery. However, despite this setback, he went to France, from where he steadily climbed the rungs of the Roman Catholic Church to become Pope Adrian IV in 1154.

St Albans Cathedral from the south-west.

The nave is amongst the longest in England at 275 feet. The arches are built in two distinctive styles, those to the east being Norman in form while those towards the west were built in the Early English style in the late twelfth century. The contrast between the two styles is very clear, the arches built in the Early English style being much lighter and more ornamental in appearance. In 1323 two of the Norman pillars in the nave collapsed during a service, causing the roof to fall in and damaging some of the other pillars. As recorded elsewhere in this book similar disasters have afflicted most medieval cathedrals at some time in their history; at St Albans it took a long time to restore the nave to its original state. A rood screen separates the nave from the quire but its niches are empty, the statues that once filled them having been removed in the sixteenth century.

The abbey survived until 1539 when, as a consequence of Henry VIII's programme to dissolve the monasteries, many of the buildings were destroyed, the king having instructed one of his military engineers – Sir Richard Lee – to undertake the work at St Albans. In 1553 the abbey church was purchased by the people of the town for the sum of £400, to serve as their parish church. Thus it remained for the next 300 years, a building in decline, only parts of which could be used. The Lady chapel housed a school during the same period.

Restoration began in earnest in the early years of the nineteenth century with Sir George Gilbert Scott leading much of the early work while in 1880 Lord Grimthorpe supervised further restoration. During this work the roof of the quire was uncovered to reveal a collection of painted insignia, some depicting royal heraldic shields and others those of saints like St Alban, St George and King Edward the Confessor. The tower, the oldest of any cathedral in England, was built in 1077 and has walls 7 feet thick made from Roman bricks. In 1870 there were fears it might collapse and a team had to work night and day over a period of four days to avert disaster. The painted ceiling of the tower dates from the fifteenth century and displays the white roses of the

The quire and high altar.

The west front of St Albans Cathedral.

House of York and the red roses of the House of Lancaster. Two early battles of the War of the Roses were fought near St Albans; in 1455, when the Yorkists were victorious, and in 1461, when the Lancastrians won. The war between these two great dynasties was finally brought to an end in 1485 when Henry Tudor, later Henry VII, defeated the Yorkist Richard III at the battle of Bosworth Field in Leicestershire. In 1950 a new tower ceiling was painted to resemble the original, which had become dilapidated with age.

The shrine of St Alban is situated east of the high altar screen and is hidden from the view of anybody in the presbytery; this was not originally so since prior to 1484 a much lower screen existed, permitting the monks to see the shrine of their patron saint when celebrating mass. The much higher altar screen was added to conform to liturgical changes but was severely damaged at the time of the Reformation, as was the reliquary containing St Albans remains, which was removed on the orders of Henry VIII. Today the shrine has been partially restored while work to refurbish the screen was undertaken at the end of the nineteenth century. Besides the central figure of Christ on the cross surrounded by the twelve apostles, are carvings of appropriate Saxon saints including one of Pope Adrian IV. At the bottom of the screen and directly above the high altar is the reredos, which depicts Christ rising from the tomb upon resurrection, with the hands of God removing his crown of thorns while two angels carry away his earthly burdens. The reredos was sculpted by Sir Alfred Gilbert, another of whose works is the statue of Eros in Piccadilly Circus.

The two transepts are largely Norman although the south transept was altered by Lord

Grimthorpe in the nineteenth century. His plans were not to everybody's satisfaction, some of his changes being thought to border upon 'vandalism'. Adjacent to the south transept is the modern chapter house, the original having been destroyed during the Reformation. As already noted, the Lady chapel at the east end of the cathedral was used as a school for a period of more than 300 years following the Reformation. In 1871 it was reconnected to the main body of the building and is used for some services today. It is a light and airy place and contains a page of the St Albans Bible, which dates from the fourteenth century.

St Albans is a small community and its abbey church, officially created a cathedral in 1877, lies at the centre of the city, surrounded by trees and open ground. The cathedral and its surrounding precincts exude an air of dignified calm, a place for quiet reflection in a busy world. There is a memorial adjacent to the outer wall of the cathedral on the north side of the nave, a simple headstone commemorating the life of Robert Runcie, Bishop of St Albans 1970-80 and Archbishop of Canterbury 1980-91 and one of St Albans's best-known and much respected recent bishops.

The grave of Archbishop Robert Runcie.

Chelmsford Cathedral

Its chequered flint work at the east end and the south porch is typical of churches of that part of England.

Look for Mark Cazalet's *Tree of Life* drawing and St Peter's Chapel commemorating those killed in recent conflicts.

Chelmsford, 40 miles north-east of London and the county town of Essex, has been an important administrative centre since the Roman period. In more recent times much of the western part of the county has seen the creation of several satellite towns, which have grown up as London's population has expanded. Parallel developments along the north bank of the Thames Estuary now herald further industrialization. The diocese of which Chelmsford Cathedral is the centre was not formed until 1914, when it was decided that a new diocese was required to meet the needs of an increasing population. Previously the religious affairs of the county had been discharged first by the Bishops of London, then for a short time from 1845 by the Bishop at Rochester and more recently by the St Albans' Diocese in 1877. Today the Chelmsford Diocese is the second most populous in England.

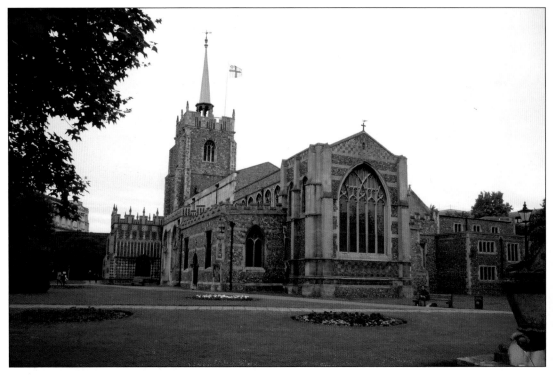

The east end of Chelmsford Cathedral.

In 653 St Cedd landed in Britain at Bradwell near the mouth of the river Blackwater, about 20 miles east of Chelmsford. Cedd was one of four brothers, two of whom became bishops: Chad, who founded Lichfield Cathedral, and Cedd, who was charged with bringing Christianity to the people of East Anglia. One of his first acts was the building of a small chapel near where he landed. This was restored in 1920 and since then has become an important place of pilgrimage. There have always been close links between the cathedral, which is dedicated to St Peter and St Cedd, and the tiny church at Bradwell.

It is not known when the first church was constructed in Chelmsford but it is thought to have been at least 800 years ago. It was largely rebuilt in the fifteenth and sixteenth centuries but suffered considerable damage at the time of the Civil War when images of Christ and the Virgin Mary were removed from the East Window. In 1641 a mob is recorded as having invaded the church, destroying what remained of the window and threatening the rector, who eventually had to flee for his life. Thereafter more damage occurred and did not cease until after the restoration of the monarchy in 1660 when order was re-established. The spire was rebuilt in 1749 with an organ installed in 1772 and bells hung in 1777. However, that was not the end of Chelmsford's problems since in 1800 the nave collapsed following the excavation of a burial vault. Further refurbishment work was carried out in the 1980s, with the chapter house being built in 1990.

Simplicity is the best word to describe the interior of today's cathedral. The small scale of the building with its whitewashed walls shows off its treasures to good effect. The East Window is, like most of the glass, nineteenth-century and depicts the Virgin Mary and eleven apostles with below them eight panels showing the life and times of Christ. The window was the gift of a former

Looking east towards the chancel.

archdeacon, St John Mildmay, who gave it in memory of his mother, the lady of the manor. The Mildmay family are closely connected with other aspects of the cathedral including the altar frontal in the chapel of the same name, which reflects the theme of pilgrimage and St Cedd's landing in Essex.

The north transept window was hidden when a new vestry was built and has been recently replaced by the *Tree of Life*, designed and painted by Mark Cazalet, a contemporary British artist. His drawing shows a vast Essex oak tree in full foliage but beginning to die back in one area. It is intended to remind people of their environment and includes references to modern phenomena such as landfill sites, thereby seeking to highlight man's disregard for his responsibilities to his fellow human beings. Also shown are biblical references to Adam and Eve, Judas Iscariot and St Cedd. The tree takes time to absorb.

There are two chapels at the western end of the cathedral, dedicated respectively to St Cedd and to St Peter. Between them, occupying space where a west window might have been, is the organ, which was rebuilt there in 1994 having previously been located in the north transept. St Peter's Chapel celebrates those who have suffered death or other misfortune in this world and contains several war memorials including a commemoration of the 'Few' who took part in the Battle of Britain in 1941. Another memorial recalls those who fought against Japan in Burma and North East India between1942 and 1945. Those immortal, anonymous words, 'When you go

The Tree of Life.

home, tell them of us and say for your tomorrow, we gave our today', are inscribed. They were originally carved on the memorial at Kohima in the former Indian state of Assam, following the epic battle fought against the Japanese in 1944. The battle was a turning point in Allied fortunes in the Far East.

Chelmsford has had close connections with America, particularly in the Second World War when before D-Day countless United States servicemen were stationed locally. In the seventeenth century Thomas Hooker, a nonconformist preacher, used to speak regularly in the Chelmsford churches. A puritan, he preached uncompromisingly about the responsibilities pertaining to government and the consensual role of the people and came to be seen as a threat by the church authorities. As a result Hooker was forced to flee the country and eventually emigrated to America, where he helped to found the state of Connecticut.

Railway Notes

Chapter 10 of this book touched briefly upon the control of train movements. One of the essential ingredients of an efficient railway network has to be the timetable that stipulates when trains should run, where they will stop and which operating company will provide which services. In the earliest days timetables were compiled by experts calculating speeds and passing points, making allowances for connections and ensuring that where a particular train was required for a return service, sufficient time was allowed for its preparation. Nowadays computer modelling has made compilation easier and quicker although, with so many different operators now involved, planning is just as complex.

A printed timetable has been an essential part of planning a train journey ever since railways came into existence. George Bradshaw in the middle of the nineteenth century was amongst the first to understand the need for accurate information and clear directions as to how and where to travel. Early timetables were difficult to read for two reasons; the lack of co-ordination between railway companies and the fact that there was no unified system of time until the latter part of the century. In addition to making sense of train times and connections Bradshaw's timetable books provided descriptions of routes and stations and suggested places that might be visited. For people previously unused to travelling more than a short distance from home his guidance greatly assisted them as they ventured to use the fast expanding and novel Victorian railway system.

Bradshaw published his first timetable in 1839. He had been born near Manchester in 1801 and spent most of his working life in that city, where he established a printing works. His name came to be known both at home and abroad as his timetables were increasingly seen as an essential accessory to travel both in Britain and overseas. He died in Norway in 1853 while visiting that country and is buried in Oslo Cathedral.

Modern timetables are more practical and contain none of the appealing embellishments included by Bradshaw. In time they too will no doubt be replaced by information provided electronically and solely through Internet websites or text messages to an individual's mobile telephone. Such developments will hasten the day when travel by train becomes less an adventure to be savoured and more a process to be completed as quickly as possible, in a world where time dictates everything.

A Docklands Light Railway train at Stratford, East London.

71000 *Duke of Gloucester*, commissioned in 1954 and one of the last steam locomotives to be built by British Railways. Now preserved. (Courtesy of Mrs Angus Thomas)

A Grand Tour

Not everyone will either have the time nor the wish to visit all the cathedrals described in the previous chapters. I have therefore constructed an itinerary that covers some of the best-known cathedrals in England, which, if visited in the order set out, would take the traveller by train just over a week. The tour follows a clockwise route first visiting the West Country, then the South Midlands and the North of England before returning to London via East Anglia. A total of fourteen cathedrals are included.

Day One Leave London Waterloo early on a South West Trains service for Exeter St David's Station, an overall journey time of under three-and-a-half hours. By using this route rather than the parallel line to the west from Paddington, it is possible to visit Salisbury Cathedral on the way and Exeter Cathedral on arrival in the West Country city. Overnight in Exeter.

Day Two Should the traveller wish they can visit Truro Cathedral by taking a Great Western train from Exeter to Truro and return, a direct service taking no more than two-and-a-half hours each way. A second overnight stay in Exeter on return.

Royal Albert Bridge.

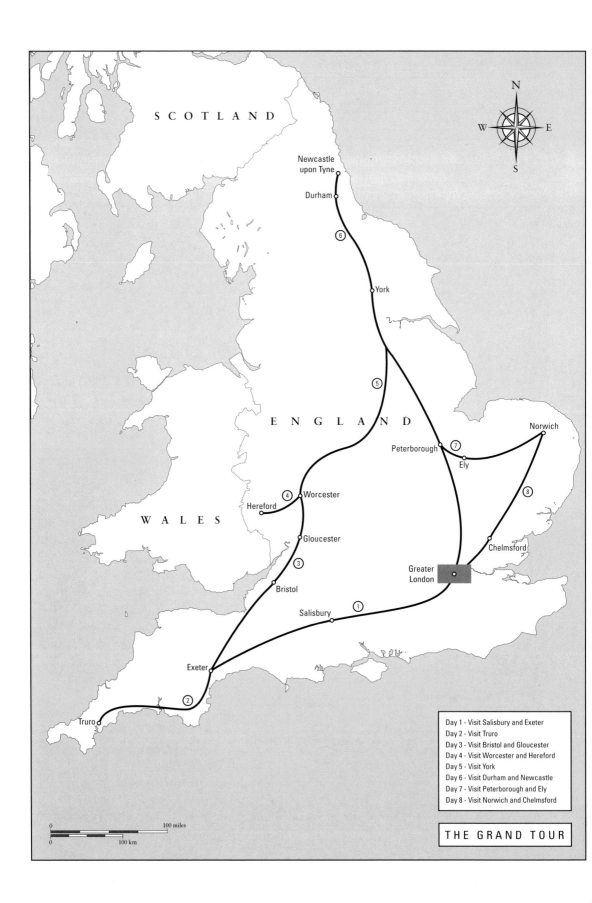

N
W • E
S

SCOTLAND

Newcastle
upon Tyne
Durham

⑥

York

⑤

ENGLAND

Norwich

Peterborough ⑦
Ely

Worcester
④
Hereford

WALES

Gloucester

③

Bristol

Chelmsford

Greater
London

Salisbury
①

Exeter

②

Truro

0   100 miles
0   100 km

Day 1 - Visit Salisbury and Exeter
Day 2 - Visit Truro
Day 3 - Visit Bristol and Gloucester
Day 4 - Visit Worcester and Hereford
Day 5 - Visit York
Day 6 - Visit Durham and Newcastle
Day 7 - Visit Peterborough and Ely
Day 8 - Visit Norwich and Chelmsford

THE GRAND TOUR

Worcester Cathedral.

Day Three By travelling on an early train from Exeter, using either a Great Western or a Cross Country service, Bristol can be reached in an hour. Following a visit to Bristol Cathedral the traveller then returns to Temple Meads Station and takes a local service to Gloucester. Having visited Gloucester Cathedral he takes another local train to Worcester, a journey of forty-five minutes. Overnight in Worcester.

Day Four Visit Worcester Cathedral and then travel to Hereford, a journey that will take less than an hour. Visit Hereford Cathedral and then return to Worcester by the same Great Western service. A second night in Worcester.

Day Five Travel from Worcester to Birmingham New Street, taking less than an hour. Change at New Street Station, the railway crossroads of Middle England, and then board an Arriva Cross Country train for York, a journey taking approximately two hours. Visit York Minster and stay overnight in York.

Day Six Head north to Durham on an East Coast or a Cross Country train and visit Durham Cathedral. The journey will take less than an hour and if the traveller wishes they can go on to Newcastle to visit Newcastle Cathedral, only twenty minutes further north. Following this visit return to York for a second night.

A High Speed Train – the workhorse of express services for much of the last forty years.

Day Seven Travel south from York to Peterborough using an East Coast service taking an hour. Visit Peterborough Cathedral and then catch an East Midlands train to Ely and Norwich. Break your journey to see Ely Cathedral and then go on to Norwich using the same service. The overall journey time from Peterborough to Norwich, discounting the time taken to visit Ely Cathedral, is under two hours. Overnight in Norwich.

Day Eight Visit Norwich Cathedral and then return to London by National Express (East Anglia), arriving at Liverpool Street Station in less than two hours. If wished this last journey could be broken at Chelmsford to visit Chelmsford Cathedral.

Summary
Nights 1 and 2 in Exeter.
Nights 3 and 4 in Worcester.
Nights 5 and 6 in York.
Night 7 in Norwich.

I am aware that some of England's greatest cathedrals are not included in my proposed itinerary. In particular, Canterbury, Lincoln and Winchester cannot be incorporated into the above plan

Steam locomotives powered the railways over much of the nineteenth and twentieth centuries. 60163 *Tornado* was privately built by the A1 Steam Locomotive Trust and first ran in 2008.

without extending travelling times disproportionately. I also regret that it has not been possible to include the two great cathedrals at Chester and Liverpool, whose stories are told in Chapters 11 and 12 respectively.

Clearly the suggested programme can be amended to suit the traveller. For example, the visit to Truro can be left out, saving a day.

I have included the names of the train companies providing the various services but not the times of individual trains. The latter can change, as of course may the identity of train companies should the Government decide to renegotiate the current operational franchises at some stage in the future. However, I doubt whether the latter would lead to a fundamental alteration to the routes I have advised, but a check with rail enquiries should be undertaken prior to travel. Ticketing is another issue I have deliberately not touched upon; again, an enquiry would be wise since multi-route 'rover' tickets at reduced rates are often available.

The west front of Norwich Cathedral.

The Place of the Martyrdom, Canterbury Cathedral.

Chichester Cathedral.

Cathedral Builders

They climbed on sketchy ladders towards God,
With winch and pulley hoisted hewn rock into heaven,
Inhabited sky with hammers, defied gravity,
Deified stone, took up God's house to meet Him.

And came down to their suppers and small beer;
Every night slept, lay with smelly wives,
Quarrelled and cuffed the children, lied,
Spat, sang, were happy or unhappy,

And every day took to the ladders again;
Impeded the rights of way of another summer's
Swallows; grew greyer, shakier, became less inclined
To fix a neighbours roof of a fine evening,

Saw naves sprout arches, clerestories soar,
Cursed the loud fancy glaziers for their luck,
Somehow escaped the plague, got rheumatism,
Decided it was time to give it up,

To leave the spire to others; and stood in the crowd
Well back from the vestments at the consecration,
Envied the fat bishop his warm boots,
Cocked up a squint eye and said, 'I bloody did that.'

Written by John Ormond, Selected Poems (Seren 1987)
by permission of the Estate of John Ormond.

Epilogue

In the dying years of the sixth century Augustine was sent by Pope Gregory the Great to bring Christianity to pagan Britain. He and his followers eventually settled at Canterbury, where Christian worship has been glorified ever since.

A little under 400 years later in 1066, and less than 50 miles from Canterbury, William of Normandy landed an invasion army on the shingle beaches near Hastings. The ensuing battle saw the defeat of the English under King Harold and the rapid consolidation of Norman rule across many parts of Britain. That was the last time that these islands were invaded.

The British have always lived their lives in the belief that the 20 miles of sea that separates them from the European mainland, provides a degree of security from invasion, a confidence well merited by the events of 1940, when perhaps the greatest national threat of all times was deterred by the waters of the English Channel.

Ironically that feeling of security implicit in the waters of the Channel evaporated for many when, in 1988, it was agreed to build an undersea tunnel to carry railway traffic between England and France, thereby establishing a land link between Britain and her European neighbours. That tunnel, completed in six years, makes its landfall in England at Folkestone, just 20 miles south of Canterbury and not quite equidistant between Canterbury and Hastings.

Had St Augustine not come to these shores Christianity might not have taken root in Britain in the way it did. Had the Norman invasion not succeeded there might have been no great medieval cathedrals. Without the technology attendant on developments in railways and civil engineering, there would be no Channel Tunnel linking Britain to Europe. These momentous events, and many similar, have helped to shape the course of British history or, in the case of the Tunnel, are set to do so.

There is a hilltop a few miles north of Dover that affords views in every direction. It offers a tranquil setting from which to contemplate the theme of this book. To the south-west lies the Channel coast around Hastings, where the Normans landed; to the north is the mighty silhouette of Canterbury Cathedral; from the west the Pilgrim's Way wends along the North Downs; to the east and south lies the coast of France. And then there is a fifth direction: beneath your feet and not far from where you are standing runs the Channel Tunnel, a railway line beyond the dreams of the Victorian railway pioneers of the nineteenth century.

History has dictated this coincidence of historical events in the south-east corner of England where invaders once landed and today travellers come and go in comfort. The Norman visionaries and the Victorian geniuses who built the cathedrals and railways of England never met one another, but they shared one vital characteristic: they were building for the future. Thanks to them, we modern pilgrims can meditate on the meaning of their labours as we travel the length and breadth of the country without becoming footsore. Take your copy of Chaucer and your Bible when you go. Cathedrals and trains are good places for a little reading.

Glossary of Cathedral Terms

Cathedral From the Latin word *cathedra*, meaning a seat. Thus a cathedral is the seat or throne of a bishop who has jurisdiction over a diocese or district that contains a number of parishes. The term 'mother church' is also used to describe a cathedral's role.

  The Archbishops of Canterbury and York have roles as diocesan bishops in addition to their wider duties in the Church of England. Their *cathedra* are located in Canterbury Cathedral and York Minster respectively.

Dean and Chapter A Chapter led by the Dean is responsible for the management of a cathedral on a day by day basis.

Minster A church or cathedral that in Anglo Saxon times was a missionary centre, a place from which the clergy would go out into the surrounding areas to enlighten people about God and the teachings of the bible. A church of any size could be termed a minster.

Layout of a cathedral Usually laid out in the form of a cross or cruciform. The crossing is the point at which the quire, nave and transepts intersect. It is often surmounted by a central tower.

Quire The eastern part of a cathedral because the choir is normally placed there. Other terms to describe this area are the presbytery, from the Latin word *presbyter*, meaning priest, or the chancel, from the Latin *cancellus*, or screen. Those occupying the quire sit in stalls; in many cathedrals these contain misericords, a form of 'tip-up' seat that allowed the occupier to rest his body when required to stand for long periods.

  The different spelling of the two words is to differentiate the place – quire – from the singers of church music – choir.

  In many cathedrals a screen separates the quire from the nave. Some screens were removed in Victorian times to give an uninterrupted view throughout a cathedral. Screens are sometimes called *pulpitum*.

Retroquire Part of the quire beyond the high altar. Also known as an ambulatory if the latter gives access to side aisles branching from it.

Nave The western end of a cathedral. The word derives from the Latin *navis*, meaning ship. In medieval times people thought of themselves as embarking in a ship and setting out to sail to meet their God when they entered the nave of a church or cathedral. Until comparatively recently naves were used more as a meeting place or venue for a variety of activities not necessarily of a religious nature. Today large cathedral services often use the nave and sometimes both the nave and the quire for services.

Nave arches These are often arranged in layers, the arcade at ground level built with the biggest arches with smaller arches in the triforium above. Above them at the top is the clerestory, designed to let light into the nave through glass windows placed in the arches.

Transepts These are the crosspieces of the cruciform and are termed the north or south transept. Side chapels are located here and transepts also provide space for processions to form up or special services to take place. Some cathedrals have more than two transepts and these are identified by their direction from the rest of the building, i.e. north-west transept, or a similar designation.

Chapels Cathedrals tend to have several chapels built on the perimeter, each usually dedicated to a particular saint. Chantry chapels were built in medieval times to permit the singing of prayers for a departed soul, usually a bishop or senior priest. Many such chapels have since been removed from most cathedrals.

Lady chapel Usually, but not always, a large chapel connected to the east end of a cathedral and dedicated to the Blessed Virgin Mary. Often used for a particular service such as the daily Eucharistic or a service of commemoration.

Apse The east end of most cathedrals is square although some are semi-circular, when the area is known as the apse.

High altar Positioned at the eastern end of the quire and within the sanctuary, the high altar is the principal altar of a cathedral and is recognized as holy with entry usually restricted to the clergy. Most cathedrals also have an altar at the east end of the nave.

Crypt From the Greek word *krypto*, meaning hidden. An underground space or vault below a cathedral. Often used as a burial place. Sometimes entered from an adjacent undercroft, where cathedrals today harness the space to exhibit church plate and other precious possessions.

Cloisters From the Latin *claustrum*, an enclosed space. Normally situated on the south side of a cathedral and a place where monks would study or follow their daily routine. Cloisters are usually, but not exclusively, associated with monastic settlements.

Chapter house A building attached to a cathedral where the priests responsible for organizing a cathedral would meet to discuss its management. The word chapter stems from the medieval custom of reading a section of the bible or some other work each day. Chapter houses are not consecrated ground and they are used for a variety of purposes including concerts, fund-raising events and receptions in addition to clergy meetings.

Architectural periods These are not precise but the Gothic period covered from the twelfth to the sixteenth centuries in Western Europe. Within this bracket the Romanesque or Norman period broadly equates to the late eleventh/early twelfth centuries, the Early English to the thirteenth century, the Decorated to the fourteenth century and the Perpendicular to the fifteenth century. These are very approximate equivalences.

Bibliography

The official guidebooks, companion guides and associated literature published for sale by the cathedrals visited.

BRYANT, Arthur, *A Thousand Years of the British Monarchy*, Collins, London, 1975.

SCOTT MONCRIEFF, M.C., *Kings and Queens of England*, Blandford Press, London, 1966.

PLATTEN, The Very Revd Stephen, *Cathedrals and Abbeys of England*, Jarrold Publishing, Andover, 1999.

STREET, Pamela, *Portrait of Witshire*, Robert Hale, London, 1971.

HEY, David, *Yorkshire from AD 1000*, Longman, London, 1986.

Book of British Towns, Drive Publications, Basingstoke, 1979.

TINDAL HART, A, *Ebor, The Archbishops of York*, Sessions Book Trust, York, 1986.

BARKWORTH, Peter, *For all Occasions, a selection of poems, prose and party pieces*, Methuen, London, 1997.

RAW, David, *It's Only Me*, Frank Peters Publishing, Kendal, 1988.

Railways

HAMILTON ELLIS, Cuthbert, *British Railway History 1877-1947*, George Allen & Unwin, London, 1959.

WOLMAR, Christian, *Fire and Steam*, Atlantic Books, London, 2007.

LE VAY, Benedict, *Britain from the Rails*, Bradt, Chalfont St Peter, 2009.

FIENNES, G.F., *I tried to run a railway*, Ian Allan, London, 1967.

ROLT, L.T.C., *Red for Danger*, Pan Books, London, 1967.

GLANCEY, Jonathan, *John Betjeman on Trains*, Methuen, London, 2006.

BRINDLE, Steven, *Brunel*, Phoenix, London, 2005.

SIMMONS, Jack, *The Birth of the Great Western Railway*, Adam & Dart, Bath, 1971.

The Reshaping of British Railways, HMSO, London, 1963.

Acknowledgements

I have received considerable support and, more importantly, sound advice in researching and writing this book. At a very early juncture one of those advising me, herself a publisher, pointed out what a tiny percentage of those writing books ever had their work published. Her remarks presented me with a personal challenge to get on and prove her wrong!

Gordon Graham, one time Chairman of Butterworths, the scientific and legal publishers, and a close friend of the last fifteen years, and his daughter, Mrs Sylvia May, a senior executive with Harper Collins have both given me unstinting, expert help. Douglas Williamson, currently in a senior position with MacMillan, volunteered to read my manuscript and, using his considerable professional skills, provided a series of 'mock ups' to show me how the book might appear in final form. Without their help, I suspect I would not have succeeded in my endeavours.

I am also grateful to David Blackburn who read the finished manuscript soon after its completion and made pertinent comments. Individual chapters were read by a number of people including, the Rt Revd Simon Barrington Ward, formerly Bishop of Coventry, Canon Jeremy Fletcher, at one time Chaplain to the Bishop of Southwell and Nottingham, Francis Baxendale, a long time friend and knowledgeable about Chichester Cathedral and Tom Burr, a guide at Wells Cathedral and another good friend. Others too have contributed and I am grateful for their guidance.

Finally I would thank the team at Pen & Sword Publishers for their help in putting together the final book. Pleasant to deal with, they made the author's task a lot easier than it might have been.

Very finally my thanks to Lord Hope of Thornes, the former Archbishop of York, for agreeing to write the Foreword.

Murray Naylor

Index

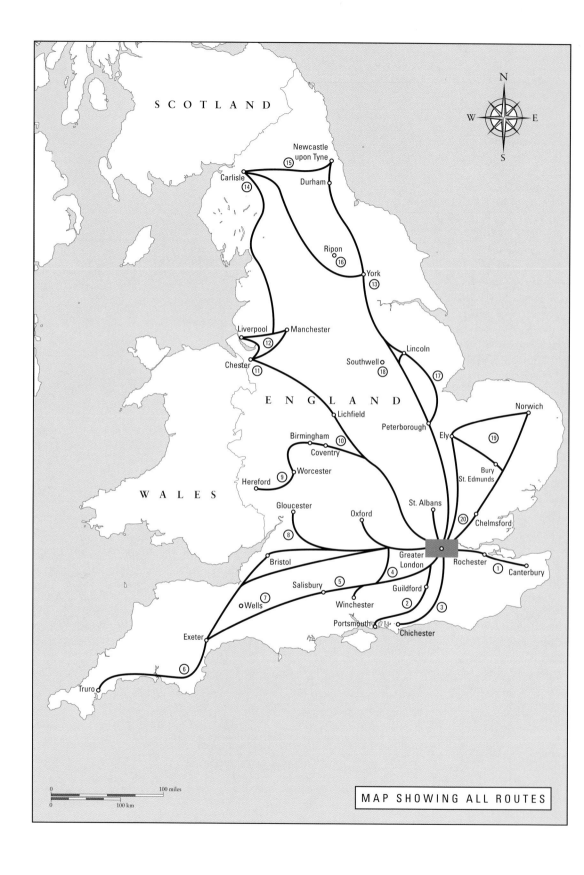

MAP SHOWING ALL ROUTES

Personal Notes